MICHELIN
FRANCE

MICHELIN
FRANCE

Landscape   Architecture   Tradition

A Bulfinch Press Book

Little, Brown and Company

Boston New York Toronto London

First Edition in 1995 by
Manufacture Française des Pneumatiques Michelin
Services de Tourisme
46 avenue de Breteuil
75324 Paris Cedex 07 France

First North American Edition

ISBN 0-8212-2219-8

Library of Congress Catalog Card Number 95-76889

Bulfinch Press is an imprint and trademark of Little, Brown and Company (Inc.)
Published simultaneously in Canada by Little, Brown and Company (Canada) Limited

Printed and Bound in Hong Kong

Contents

Foreword

EVERYBODY knows that vague sense of anticlimax after a wonderful holiday... The long-awaited trip to France is over, the travel guides and road maps neatly returned to the bookshelves ready for the next adventure, and the reluctant home-comers are left with a feeling of nostalgia for the variety of sights, sounds and gastronomic sensations with which they have been assailed over the last few days, as they cross their fingers and wait for the holiday photographs to be developed.

For nigh on a century, Michelin has been producing travel guides. The distinctive green cover is a familiar sight as tourists consult the Michelin guide to find out where to go and what is of special interest when you get there. Detailed descriptions of places to visit are presented within their historical and cultural context and backed up by sound practical information, maps and illustrations.

Recently, it has been felt at Michelin that the time was right to complement the series of Green Guides to the regions of France with a book in which the atmosphere of a holiday in France might be captured first and foremost in full-colour images. How often do we struggle to catch those fleeting, but memorable, impressions on film ourselves – the cool reflection of a château in river or lake, brightly coloured displays of flowers or fresh local produce at a market, the warm tones of stone farmhouses or village churches, elegant and intricate cathedrals, mysterious shadows in the depths of a spectacular river gorge or jagged mountain

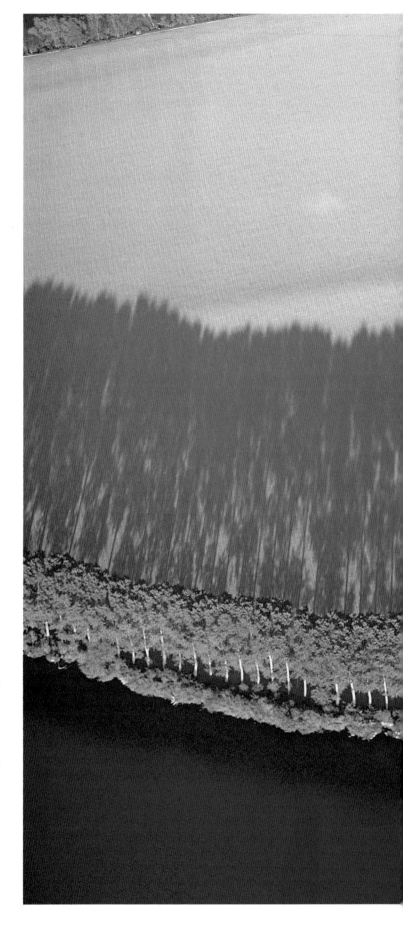

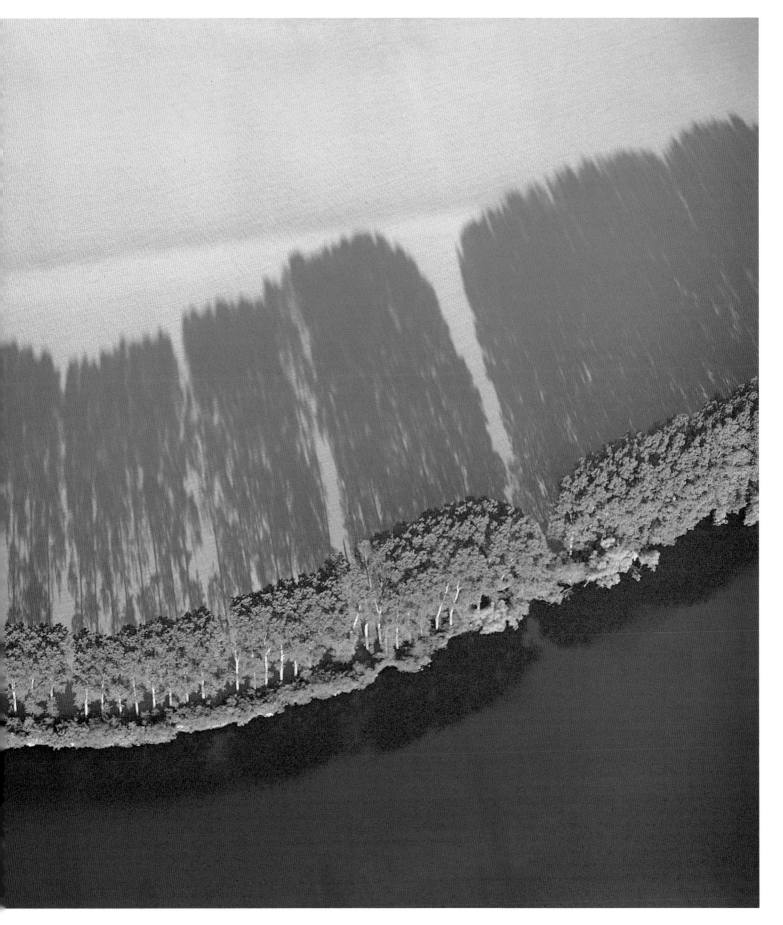

peaks etched against an azure sky? With this in mind, the photographs in this book have been selected, in collaboration with Quadrille Publishing, for the atmosphere they evoke through light and colour.

The Michelin travel writers have warmly embraced the chance to adopt a more lyrical turn of phrase than usual to celebrate the unique character and flavour of their native or adopted region in a brief descriptive text accompanying each chapter.

We hope, therefore, that the finished book will transport readers back to their holiday world, recapturing some of those aspects of France which struck a chord in them while they were there.

Michelin Green Guides

Normandy

The Cotentin, a finger of land pointing to the open sea, and the ports along the Seine estuary open Normandy up to the exterior. At the same time, its rich pastoral countryside and ancient village customs shape a region that is largely untouched by time.

The landscape and its people

COASTAL FISHING.

(ABOVE) Images of the Normandy landscape, with its orchards of flowering apple trees, hedgerows, thatched cottages and cattle raised on rich pastures sprayed by the sea mists.

(OPPOSITE) In the Pays d'Auge, the charming half-timbered manor house of Coupesarte reflected in the still waters of its moat.

MONT-ST-MICHEL, rising out of the mouth of the Couesnon river in south-west Normandy, is the symbol of Normandy and has been described as a 'wonder of the Western world'.

Like the pilgrims of old, visitors making the approach on foot, across the couple of kilometres of dike which at low tide separates the granite mound from the mainland of France, have time to contemplate the boldness of the architecture and the religious significance of this extraordinary site. The blue of the slate roofs huddled against the granite-grey rocks, the pale gold of the sandy bay, the light green of the river banks and the darker green of the few trees defiantly clinging to the ramparts combine to make the experience unforgettable.

These half-tone colours are also characteristic of the traditional Normandy landscape of wooded hillsides and fertile valleys, where the seductive outline of a château or manor house lends a note of prosperity and order.

The Cotentin peninsula in Lower Normandy resembles neighbouring Brittany. Its austere granite coastline juts out into the English Channel, powerful tides surge round the Chaussey Islands and there are maritime activities in the small fishing ports. The Normandy *bocage* is a countryside of enclosed fields, well-tended hedges, scattered farmhouses, deep lanes, dense woods and apple orchards, which burst into blossom in spring.

The Seine valley to the east is the focus for all the important channels of commerce in Upper Normandy. Standing at its central axis is Rouen, capital of the region. To the south lies the Pays d'Auge, the heart of the *bocage* country, celebrated for its ciders, cheeses, Calvados and elegant manor houses. To the north of the Seine spreads the fertile chalk plain of the Pays de Caux, where rich agricultural farmlands create oases of green. From here the land drops down to the sea in a succession of spectacular hanging valleys (*valleuses*) and white limestone cliffs, which give it the name of the Côte d'Albâtre (alabaster coast).

An eminent civilization

The reminders of Normandy's long and colourful history are everywhere. They can be seen in the Rue du Gros-Horloge and the magnificent Gothic cathedral in Rouen's old town, in the spiritual ruins of the abbey of Notre-Dame-de-Jumièges, in the

formidable twelfth-century fortress of Richard Coeur-de-Lion at Les Andelys, and in the perfect High Gothic chancel of the cathedral at Coutances. The numerous other architectural monuments and sites which punctuate the Normandy coast and countryside tell, in the most vivid way possible, the great history of this province.

Before the threatened Viking invasions in the ninth century, the area that is modern Normandy had for several centuries already been subjected to Saxon influence on the islands and along the coast, and to Frankish domination inland. In 911 the treaty of St-Clair-sur-Epte between the French king Charles the Simple and the Norse chieftain Rollo created, in effect, the Duchy of Normandy. From that time, the combination of the Viking spirit of adventure and negotiating skill with the Frankish strengths of rural and ecclesiastical administration was to forge a powerful and stable state. Over the next two hundred years it flourished with an exceptional brilliance, reaching the peak of its civilization in the eleventh century.

When William Duke of Normandy — staking his claim to the English throne promised him by his cousin Edward the Confessor — won a decisive victory over his rival Harold at the battle of Hastings in 1066, a new Anglo-Norman kingdom was born. On Christmas Day 1066, William was crowned King of England in Westminster Abbey.

The Bayeux Tapestry, the long series of embroideries on display in Bayeux, provides a remarkably detailed contemporary account of the Norman conquest, as well as a precise record of the ships, weapons, clothes and way of life of the Middle Ages. The origin of this artistic masterpiece is uncertain: no longer attributed to Queen Matilda, it is now thought to have been commissioned by Odo, Bishop of Bayeux, and made by Saxon weavers in England.

A century later, the Plantagenet kingdom of Henry II of England, a distant heir of William the Conqueror, was to stretch from the river Tweed on the Scottish border to Bayonne near the border of Spain.

The great Norman abbeys

The majestic architecture of the abbey churches at Le Bec-Helllouin, Caen, Fécamp, Hambye, Lessay, Jumièges, Mont-St-Michel, St-Georges-de-Boscherville, St-Ouen and St-Wandrille shows the extent of the Duchy's monastic wealth and influence in the Middle Ages.

(*ABOVE*) *Detail of one of the fifty-eight scenes from the famous Bayeux Tapestry, on display in the Centre Guillaume le Conquérant in Bayeux.*

(*RIGHT*) *In its day the abbey of Bec-Helllouin, as famous as that of Jumièges, was one of the great intellectual centres of the West. Today it is still a place of Christian contemplation, study and meetings.*

Of all these places, the great Notre-Dame-de-Jumièges has perhaps the most awe-inspiring and spiritual atmosphere. Today, the harsh croaks of its jackdaw colony have replaced the plainsong of earlier days, but it does not take much imagination to transform this evocative site into the glorious place of worship that, at its height of splendour, housed some 700 monks and 1,500 lay brothers. The two tall eleventh-century towers are open to the elements, as are the four stately double bays of the nave. The sight of the remaining wall of the lantern tower and the bases of the chancel, ambulatory and axial chapel walls makes a deep impression.

At Caen, the Abbayes aux Hommes and aux Dames were founded by William Duke of Normandy and his wife Matilda. When William had first asked for the hand of Matilda of Flanders, she had rebuffed him. Furious, he had stormed to Lille and delivered a magisterial rebuke to the proud Matilda, who finally consented. The pope, however, disapproving of their distant kinship, excommunicated the couple and called for an interdiction on the whole of Normandy. In 1059, after the intervention of Lanfranc, the sanctions were lifted and William and Matilda made amends by building these two churches, one for the monks and the other for the nuns.

The church of St-Étienne, for the monks, was built between 1066 and 1078. The austerity of the plain west front is transformed by the magnificence of the two slim towers that sweep upwards. Inside, the immense nave is a fine example of Romanesque construction. The great lantern tower, probably designed by its first abbot, Lanfranc, is a masterpiece of balance, proportion and line. The chancel, one of the earliest examples of the Norman Gothic style, served as a model for a number of other buildings in the Duchy, notably the cathedral at Coutances.

Mont-St-Michel is unique in its setting, the wealth of its history, the beauty of its architecture and the extent of its influence. The abbey was reconstructed, after a fire, in the early thirteenth century in the triumphant Gothic style. On the north side of the mount is the group of buildings known as the Merveille; at the centre are the cloisters, with their slim, pink granite columns arranged in a quincunx pattern enclosing a fairy-tale garden.

Despite being besieged more than once during the Hundred Years War, the most sombre period in France's history, Mont-St-Michel survived as the only part of north-western France not to fall into English hands: its guardian Archangel St Michael was vigilant. Joan of Arc chose 'St-Michel-Montjoie!' as her rallying cry against the British, and in 1469 Louis XI founded the Order of St Michael.

(TOP) Abbaye de St-Wandrille: detail of the impressive pillars, the remains of the thirteenth-century Gothic abbey.

(ABOVE AND LEFT) Abbaye de Jumièges: the wall of the transept separating the nave from the choir, and the view of the nave and the large gallery opening on to it.

(OPPOSITE) Aerial view of the Abbaye du Mont-St-Michel: in the foreground the façade looking over the western platform and, farther to the left, the cloisters and buildings of the Merveille.

(LEFT) Château de Victot:
a magnificent example of late
sixteenth-century Norman
architecture in which brick, stone
and glazed tiles blend in harmony.

(ABOVE) Interiors of dovecotes:
the number of pigeon-holes varied
according to the wealth of the
proprietor.

In the midst of woods and meadows, the stud farm of Le Pin, whose buildings were designed by Mansart, provides a stately home to the élite of French horsebreeding.

The charms of the Pays d'Auge lie in its manor houses, thatched cottages and isolated farmhouses surrounded by apple orchards. Half-timbered buildings, spread around the the main living quarters, accommodate the apple store, the press — whose heavy millstone crushes the apples to cider — the stables and the all-important dairy.

A natural cornucopia

NORMANDY is a region of abundance: though rugged in places, the fertile ground yields rich harvests from land and sea. The gentle life is evoked in the vision of apple orchards in full bloom, green pastures and a profusion of milk and cream. Centuries of expertise lie behind some of Normandy's most popular dairy products: Isigny butter and Camembert, Livarot, Pont-l'Évêque and Neufchâtel cheeses.

Besides the mainstay of cream, traditional dishes almost invariably include apples in some form, and flambéed cider or Calvados is often used to add a subtle smack to smooth, creamy sauces. Sheep that have grazed on the salty coastal grass beside the bay of Mont-St-Michel or along the mud banks near Portbail are prized for their tender, delicately flavoured meat, known as *mouton de pré-salé*. Local seafood includes crabs, clams ('Venus clams' to connoisseurs), prawns and oysters from Courseulles or St-Vaast-La-Hougue. Freshly caught fish is often served in a rich creamy *sauce normande*, sometimes with the addition of mushrooms.

In Normandy, winter merges into summer, just as the land unites with the sea. Flowers bloom as if it were April all the year round. On the coast the golden yellow of spring gorse gradually gives way to the autumnal tints of purple heather and the russet hues of bracken. Rainfall keeps the grass of moors, fields and lawns looking astonishingly fresh and green.

The mild climate is perfect for the raising of stock, and more particularly for the noble tradition of horse-breeding. Normandy's stud farms breed French trotters, French saddle horses, Anglo-Arabs, Norman cobs, Percherons and the thoroughbreds descended from Asian stallions and English mares that are known for their elegance and speed.

Two of the most famous horse-breeding establishments in France are the stud farms of St-Lô in the Cotentin peninsula and Le Pin, which was founded in 1665, on the border of the Auge region.

A seafaring people

DETAIL OF A MEDIEVAL
FAÇADE, ROUEN

THE Normandy coastline has great variety. Around Étretat (with its famous solitary off-shore needle rock), Fécamp and Pourville-sur-Mer, there are spectacular chalk cliffs hung with valleys, giving them a scalloped appearance. Farther west are the beaches of the Côte de Nacre (mother-of-pearl coast) where the Allies landed on D-Day 1944 in the first phase of the Battle of Normandy. On the far side of the Cotentin peninsula is a desolate beach in the bay of Écalgrain. Beyond the craggy promontory known as the Nez de Jobourg lies the bight of Vauville and, separated by grassy depressions known as *mielles*, the dunes of Hatainville and Carteret. At the southernmost point of this coastline rises the majestic mound of Mont-St-Michel. Around the coastal harbours fishing fleets set sail from port, ferries ply between the coast and islands, swimmers take to the sea and anglers cast their fishing lines.

The Seine provides Paris with its vital commercial link to the sea as it flows on through Rouen to the port at Le Havre. Rising in Burgundy, just north of Dijon, the river flows across the Île-de-France, through the heart of Paris, towards Normandy. For the final hundred kilometres, before it empties into the English Channel, it snakes in a magnificent series of broad meanderings. The scenery, monuments and cultural history along this stretch of the Seine Valley make it the main tourist attraction of inland Normandy.

Normandy boasts a long line of adventurers and sailors. William the Conqueror set sail across the Channel from Dives-sur-Mer; other local heroes include Samuel de Champlain, the Dieppe shipbuilder and founder of Quebec, the Cavalier de la Salle, who took possession of Louisiana in 1682, and Jean Ango, shipbuilder and naval adviser to François I. The wealth and fame of such ports as Dieppe, Rouen, Fécamp and Granville were founded on the great seafaring expeditions to the New World.

Rouen, the capital of the region, contains some of the most beautiful examples of French Gothic architecture in France. Its huge cathedral (built between the thirteenth and sixteenth centuries) is famous for its striking nave with eleven bays beneath a magnificent sexpartite vaulted roof, bold lantern tower and perfectly proportioned chancel. Leading off the Rues du Gros-Horloge and St-Romain, and around the neighbouring Gothic church of St-Maclou in the heart of the old town, the narrow, picturesque streets are tightly packed with half-timbered houses. Steeped in history, Rouen is today a major port and a dynamic city which, for all its proximity to Paris, has preserved an identity of its own.

Whereas once the fame of Normandy was carried far and wide across the globe by its seafarers, by an irony of history the beaches of Normandy were the theatre for foreign operations during the Second World War, when, in June 1944, British, American and Canadian troops landed to begin the liberation of occupied France.

(LEFT) The cliffs of Étretat, whose jagged outline against sea and sky has been a favourite subject for painters.

(OPPOSITE) The nave of Rouen Cathedral, impressive for the purity of its soaring vertical lines.

Seaside resorts

NORMANDY'S elegant seaside resorts were once the haunt of aristocrats, the rich and those whose fragile constitutions demanded bracing sea air. Nowadays these resorts cultivate a more popular, but none the less stylish, appeal. Fashions and games may have changed since Marcel sat watching Albertine at play in Proust's *À la recherche du temps perdu*, but the beaches of Normandy still have plenty of distractions for those who like being by the sea.

In the nineteenth century, the vogue for seaside visits drew numerous artists, writers and society figures to the Normandy coast. The newly opened railways brought Paris closer to the sea, and hotels, casinos and villas sprang up in the brand new resorts of Cabourg, Deauville, Houlgate, Le Tréport and Trouville. Here styles of Norman architecture can be seen at their most exuberant – asymmetrical roofs, numerous windows and dormers – and in a wide variety of building materials, including local stone, bricks and half-timbering. Dieppe, the oldest of the resorts, attracted the wealthiest of these seaside visitors, eager to display their finery at the casinos and along the sea front; other patrons of the town included Louis-Philippe, Napoleon III, Eugène Delacroix, Saint-Saëns and Oscar Wilde.

At Deauville, as at Trouville, fashionable Parisian society still dresses up to parade along the '*planches*', the wooden

(TOP) An elegant seaside villa, a style of architecture dating from Trouville's great era as a fashionable resort.

(ABOVE) Deauville's famous casino is the focus for the annual festivities.

(LEFT) In the seaside resorts of the Côte Fleurie, famous for its fine sand, the pleasures of the beach can be combined with more cultured activities.

planks that form the promenade along the sandy beach. Deauville's world-wide reputation as the smartest resort owes as much to the luxury and sophistication of its setting as to the elegance of its year-round entertainment – flat racing and steeplechasing, the famous Grand Prix, the international yearlings sales, golf, polo and tennis tournaments, and the American film festival.

(ABOVE) Deauville beach, summer. The multicoloured parasols, waiting in the early morning for the sun-worshippers, seem to be warding off the menace of the odd grey cloud.

Cradle of Impressionism

I n the late nineteenth century, Normandy became the focus
for numerous artists for whom the landscape of subtle light,
drifting clouds, sea mists blowing off the Channel, sky and sea
at low tide, boats stranded at their moorings, long stretches of
sand and harbour life was a source of inspiration.

Just as the wild countryside around La Hague features in
the early works of Jean-François Millet, born on this far-flung
cape of the Cotentin peninsula, so many Norman towns
provided subject material for the Impressionists. Rouen and
Giverny were immortalized in the paintings of Monet. The
harbour at Le Havre appears repeatedly in the work of Corot,
Pissarro, Boudin and Monet, whose *Impression: Sunrise* (1872)
gave the movement its name.

The peaceful charm of the tiny port of Honfleur attracted a
succession of painters and Trouville was host to most of the
Impressionists at some point. The magnificent seascape and
plunging cliffs of Étretat, then a simple fishing village, inspired
many canvases by Boudin, Eugène Isabey and Monet, a
frequent visitor.

(LEFT) L'Hôtel des Roches Noires à
Trouville, *by Monet, Musée d'Orsay,
Paris.*

*(ABOVE) In his water garden at
Giverny, Monet sought to recreate the
rich atmospheric colours of the
Japanese prints he liked to collect.
Bridges hung with wisteria span his
famous water-lily pond.*

So how does one begin to capture the essence of Normandy? It is found in the cities of Rouen and Caen, in the magnificent Norman abbeys, and in Mont-St-Michel. But that is not the whole story. The spirit of Normandy also flourishes in the great bustling ports of Le Havre and Cherbourg, in the exuberant Gothic country châteaux, in the Renaissance mansions and town houses, in the fortified churches with resplendent stained glass windows, in the magnificent timberwork of covered markets (notably at St-Pierre-en-Dives) and in the world-famous museum collections.

It takes time and patience, plus a dash of the local spirit of adventure, to discover many of the nuances of this fascinating region. Wandering along the tiny country roads, off the beaten track, you may suddenly find a manor-house or dovecote half hidden from view or come upon an ancient farmhouse. It is, however, in a typical country inn, decorated with red and white check curtains and hung with old brass and pottery, that you will meet the warm welcome and friendliness that sums up the spirit of the people of Normandy.

Brittany

A land of legends and fervent faith, where megaliths, chapels and Calvaries stand out in strange silhouettes; of peaceful islands and unusual seascapes, as on the rose-coloured Côte de Granit punctuated by fantastic rock formations.

THE ROCKS OF ROTHÉNEUF, SCULPTED BY THE
NINETEENTH-CENTURY ABBOT FOURÉ.

Brittany's jagged coastline, with its long snout jutting out into the open sea, stretches for more than 1,000 kilometres along the Channel in the north, round to the Atlantic Ocean in the south. The *Armor*, the 'country near the sea', borders the now only partially forested interior or *Argoat*, the 'country of the wood'. The slow process of erosion, which has worn away the high mountains in the coastal area of Brittany's ancient Armorican Massif, has resulted in an inland landscape of gently sloping hills culminating in the Toussaines beacon – Tuchenn Gador – in the Monts d'Arrée.

The ceaseless movement of the ocean has shaped the Breton coast into the great diversity of shorelines that is the region's particular feature. From the bay of Mont-St-Michel to the Loire estuary, the coastline alternates between beaches, creeks, indented rocky shores, capes and cliffs continuously battered by pounding waves. There are immense natural anchorages and sheltered fishing harbours, as well as island refuges for seabirds and vast stretches of sandy beaches much prized by holiday-makers. Sometimes hospitable, sometimes austere and hostile, the Breton shores have a rugged beauty dominated by the changing tides.

The peninsula's most typical seascapes are along the north and west coasts. The Côte d'Émeraude (emerald coast), the name given to the coastline between the Pointe du Grouin

(OPPOSITE) The severe beauty of the Cap de la Chèvre, Crozon peninsula.

(BELOW LEFT) Granite house, Côte d'Armor.

(BELOW RIGHT) Pointe de la Torche, Baie d'Audierne, Finistère.

north of Cancale and Le Val-André, consists of a series of headlands projecting into the sea with wonderful panoramic views. Its seaside resorts include St-Malo, famous for its ramparts and naval heroes, Paramé, fashionable Dinard, long popular with the British, St-Lunaire, St-Cast-le-Guildo, Sables-d'Or-les-Pins, Erquy and Le Val-André itself. The red sandstone promontory of Cap Fréhel, a windswept, wave-battered jumble of cliffs dropping sheer into the sea, is one of the most impressive sights on this part of the coast.

Farther east, from the Pointe de l'Arcouest via Port-Blanc and Perros-Guirec to Trébeurden, the pink granite coastline has enormous strangely shaped boulders which seem to defy the law of gravity. The local inhabitants have christened them with such names as 'Napoleon's Hat', 'Death's-Head', 'Ram' and 'Corkscrew'. The mild climate in this region encourages a varied vegetation: lush flowering shrubs are a feast for the eyes, and magnificent bushes of blue, pink and purple hydrangeas, flowering in small patches of garden, brighten up the façades of the granite houses.

In north-west Finistère (*finis terra*, 'the end of the earth'), the typically severe, sometimes wild, coast is broken up by estuaries (*abers*) such as Aber-Wrac'h, Aber-Benoît and Aber-Ildut. These estuaries, which look magnificent at high tide, cut deeply into the coastal plateau. Still known as the Côte des Légendes (coast of legends), this bleak stretch of coastline serves as a reminder that the ocean is not only a source of

(ABOVE) Fishing occupies a central place in Breton life. On the coast, all along the seashore, it follows the rhythm of the tides. Deep-sea fishing with nets takes place in the gulf of Gascony, in the Irish Sea and off Iceland. The tuna fishermen, along the coast of Africa, use long nets called sennes. *Shellfish are caught off the rocky coastlines by means of special pots.*

(OPPOSITE) Oyster-farming is a very important economic activity. A major producer of flat oysters called belons, *Brittany has also developed the farming of a special type of deep-shelled oyster marketed as* creuses de Bretagne *or* fines de Bretagne.
The Atlantic coast has a number of important fishing ports, to which the trawlers return accompanied by the cries of greedy seagulls.

riches but also the harbinger of death, shipwreck, dirt and pollution. In the south of the Finistère *département*, at the Pointe de Penhir on the Crozon peninsula and at the Pointe du Raz, the sea and coast are seen at the height of their grim beauty: the cliffs have a giddy steepness, the rocks are pinkish grey in colour and the sea breaks with fury on the reefs. The sinister ring of local place names – Baie des Trépassés (bay of the dead) and Enfer de Plogoff (Plogoff inferno) – reflects the savage setting and the raging elements.

The town of Brest is protected by its anchorage linked to the Atlantic through a narrow channel. Established as the maritime capital of Brittany by Colbert, the great seventeenth-century minister of the French navy, Brest still plays a strategic role in France's defence policy, with aircraft carriers and nuclear submarines sheltering in its harbour. Opposite Brest, on the Cornouaille coast, Douarnenez is set deep in an immense bay with gently curving shores. One of the busiest Breton fishing ports, it is a great centre of the canning industry as well as a seaside resort. In the Port-Musée, trawlers and tuna boats lie moored alongside fishing boats for spiny lobster and shellfish in a display of the town's maritime past.

In contrast to the rocky headlands, the southern coastline of Brittany is often low-lying. The inhospitable bay of Audierne, the coast between Lorient and the Quiberon peninsula, the Morbihan beaches and the sea-front of La Baule all give a foretaste of the great expanses of sand which predominate south of the Loire.

Along the southern Finistère coast and the gulf of Morbihan there are some important fishing ports, including Audierne, Guilvinec, Lesconil, Loctudy, Concarneau, Lorient and Etel. Here the fleets bring in catches of crayfish, prawns, lobster, tuna, sole, skate and sea-bream – delicacies which, with other shellfish and oysters, are delicious served with a chilled Breton Muscadet or Gros Plant du Pays Nantais. The 'little inland sea' of the Morbihan gulf is dotted with a multitude of small islands which can be visited by boat from Vannes, Port-Navalo, Auray or Locmariaquer, with its great isolated stone menhir at the entrance to the gulf. The exceptional scenery, light and microclimate make the gulf one of Brittany's most prized spots.

The Château de Suscinio was, in the old days, the summer residence of the dukes of Brittany. To the south, the walled town of Guérande stands on a plateau overlooking the low-lying pastures of the Brière regional park and the salt marshes. Up until the fifteenth century, Guérande exported salt which was particularly rich in mineral salts to the Baltic Sea; today salt is still produced in the immense patchwork of saltpans. Beyond them, in a magnificent bay, lies the famous sea-front of La Baule. This elegant promenade, in a seven-kilometre stretch from west to east between Le Pouligen and Pornichet, is now a popular resort lined with luxury hotels, thalassotherapy centres, sports clubs and a casino.

Brittany's islands

A PEACEFUL SCENE AT POULDU.

BRITTANY'S islands, where bracing winds blow almost all the year round, are refuges of peace. Bréhat's scalloped coastline is surrounded by thousands of smaller islands with pink rocks and reefs which emerge from an emerald sea. The mild climate allows delicate mimosa, eucalyptus, fig trees, agapanthus and hydrangeas to flourish. Part of the charm of Bréhat is that the island can only be explored on foot or by bicycle.

Ushant, the westernmost point of France, is an island of ferocious winds, frequent fogs, countless reefs and strong currents which make navigation in the area notoriously

(ABOVE) The 'needles' of Port-Coton, Belle-Île. These pyramids of rock, pierced by grottoes and battered by the waves, are one of the principal attractions of the island's Côte Sauvage.

(OPPOSITE) Le Palais, the little capital of Belle-Île, a charming Breton harbour where ferries and fishing vessels are moored below the citadel.

Ushant, which is part of the Armorique regional nature park, has preserved its traditional character. At the hamlet of Niou Uhella, two houses in vernacular style have interiors that are typical of the island. The wooden furniture is made of pieces of flotsam, and is painted blue to symbolize the protection of the Virgin.

dangerous for sailors. There have been many shipwrecks around Ushant's rocks in the past. In the summer months, however, the weather is calmer and the detour to visit the main town of Lampoul, the brightly coloured fishermen's houses, the wild coast, the colonies of seabirds and the delightful little creeks is well worth making.

Groix, a schist plateau rising to a modest height, has a wild, indented coastline along its northern and western shores. Elsewhere the land is flatter, with sheltered sandy creeks like the Pointe des Chats, the lowest point of the island.

Belle-Île, Brittany's largest island, shares the same geological formation as Groix. As an outlying stronghold, it was subject to attack by British and Dutch fleets throughout the centuries. The island's highly sophisticated defences can be seen in the citadel of Le Palais, the capital, and in several isolated fortifications standing sentinel along the coast. The windswept centre of the island is a mass of wheat fields alternating with patches of yellow gorse. Small sheltered valleys, lush fields and clusters of whitewashed houses contrast with the wild southern coastline, indented with tall rocks and the pyramid-shaped Port-Coton 'needles' where the sea bubbles and swells in a great mass of fleecy foam.

The Argoat

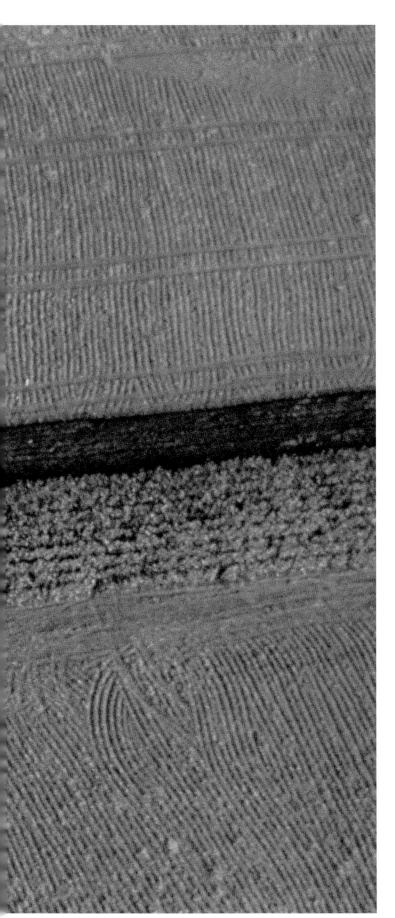

LACE HEADDRESS AND STARCHED
COLLAR, PONT AVEN.

A LTHOUGH less picturesque than the *Armor*, the Breton interior is just as attractive, and lends itself to long walks. For those who take the time to look, admire and wander, the *Argoat* is a rich and spellbinding region. Once densely forested, it is now a mixture of scattered woods and bleak moorland. The Forêt de Paimpont – famous in romantic medieval legend as the abode of the sorcerer Merlin and the fairy Viviane – is all that remains of the Armorican Massif's original forest. Sadly disfigured by a terrible fire, it is slowly coming back to life. Where once there were ancient beeches and oaks, now gorse, heather, broom and fern have shaped a new landscape which is wonderful for nature lovers to explore.

The countryside between the Noires and Arrée mountains is broken, hilly and often mysterious when mist shrouds the summits. In spite of its relatively low altitude, this part of central Brittany seems to be higher because of the barrenness and loneliness of the windswept crests looming over the undulating plains. In clear weather there is a wonderful view from Ménez Hom – the highest point in the Montagnes Noires – taking in a vast expanse from the bay of Douarnenez to the plateau of Finistère.

The Monts d'Arrée, the higher mountain range between the province of Léon in the north and Cornouaille in the south, form part of the Armorique regional nature park. The appeal of these untamed heights lies in their desolateness. Here erosion has turned summits of the rocky massif into rounded hills (*menez*) or sharp crests fretted into saw-teeth and bristling with needles (*roc'hs*), such as Roc Trévezel. Covered in gorse which resembles an immense cloak of gold in spring, the land turns purple in September when the heather is in flower. Around the forested area of Huelgoat, trees, lake, underground rivers and rocks combine to make this one of the finest resorts in inland Brittany.

(OPPOSITE) Brittany is a major agricultural region. Cereal crops cover a third of the worked land and are grown alongside forage plants (principally maize) for stock. The damp and sheltered coastal regions of the so-called 'golden belt' are devoted to market gardening. Cabbages, potatoes, artichokes, cauliflowers, shallots and onions are grown in open fields.

Megaliths and religious zeal

THE megaliths in the gulf of Morbihan — and in particular around Carnac, Locmariaquer, Monteneuf and the Île de Gavrinis — represent an astonishing journey back into the mists of time. They belong to a little-known civilization that preceded the Gauls, probably between 5000 and 2000 BC. For centuries these stone monuments — menhirs, alignments, flat-topped dolmens, cairns and covered alleyways — were associated with the mystic life of the people of Brittany. Particularly mysterious, however, is their arrangement of lines, which has given rise to various different interpretations. Today the debate about whether they are astronomical landmarks, remains of religious monuments or funerary chambers still continues. But perhaps the most perplexing question that no one has yet been able to answer is how these enormous blocks of stone, which weigh up to 350 tons, were moved and set upright in the first place.

ROOD SCREEN, A TRACERY IN WOOD,
THE CHAPEL OF ST-FIACRE, LE FAOUËT.

Brittany has an impressive number of more recent religious monuments erected mainly during the reign of Anne of Brittany, and particularly after her marriage to Charles VIII in 1491. Even the smallest town and village manifests the popular devotion, having its own church or chapel built by the local people and designed by artists who put into their works all the faith that inspired them. The sculpture of altarpieces, capitals and rood screens displays great freshness and originality. The rood screens, which are of unparalleled richness, are occasionally sculpted in granite, as in the church at Le Folgoët, but are more typically carved in wood, as in the chapel of St-Fiacre near Le Faouët.

The parish close, or enclosure, is typical of Breton communities. In Lower Brittany many were built during the sixteenth and seventeenth centuries. Neighbouring villages rivalled each other in their extravagance, with competition sometimes going on for two hundred years. These closes usually consist of a monumental gateway or triumphal arch to the cemetery, a church with its small square (*placître*), a charnel house and a monumental Calvary. These elaborately chiselled Calvaries represent episodes of the Passion around Christ on the Cross. The sculpture, sometimes rough and naïve, is strikingly lifelike and expressive; the finest examples are at Guimiliau, Plougastel-Daoulas, Pleyben, St-Thégonnec and Notre-Dame-de-Tronoën.

While these monuments reveal the intensity of religious faith, so do the regular *pardons* or processions to churches and chapels, dedicated to local saints, throughout Brittany. The faithful make pilgrimages to seek forgiveness for their sins, to realize the fulfilment of a vow or to make a plea for grace.

The procession, which takes place in the afternoon, is a colourful ceremony: candles, banners and gilded statues of saints are carried by men and women often in traditional costume, and a priest carrying the Blessed Sacrament is followed by pilgrims singing hymns. Some of the most impressive *pardons* are those of St Yves at Tréguier, the *Grand Pardon* of Ste-Anne-d'Auray and the *Troménies* at Locronan.

(ABOVE) Dedicated to the Virgin or to Breton saints, the annual pardons *draw enormous numbers of the faithful.*

(OPPOSITE) Brittany's long and close links with religion can be seen in the wealth of its stone monuments and religious buildings. Richly decorated churches and rural chapels are expressions of popular faith and local pride.

(LEFT) Decorative motifs on altars are carved with great flair.

Historic cities

RENNES, the capital of Brittany, is a city of contrasts. The old quarter, with its narrow winding streets and neat timber houses that survived the fire of 1720, retains its medieval atmosphere. The public buildings and private mansions of the two royal squares, on the other hand, display an elegant eighteenth-century solemnity. The old Parliament of Brittany alternated between Rennes and Nantes before settling definitively in Rennes in 1561, during the reign of Henri IV. The splendid stone mansion (now the Law Courts) that housed it was seriously damaged by a fire in February 1994.

Nantes, the historic capital of the duchy and birthplace of Anne of Brittany, still boasts the mid-fifteenth-century castle which served both as fortress and palace. Here, in 1598, Henri IV signed the Edict of Nantes which was intended to settle the religious question by acknowledging the Protestant religion. In the eighteenth century the city became extremely prosperous. Wealthy ship-owners who had made their money out of sugar and the slave or 'ebony' trade, as it was euphemistically known, built impressive houses with wrought-iron balconies on the former Île Feydeau where the celebrated writer Jules Verne was born in 1828.

The name St-Malo conjures up the sea and the exploits of its seamen such as Jacques Cartier, who discovered Canada, and enterprising privateers like Duguay-Trouin and Surcouf. The old walled city, with its granite mansions, tall chimneys and steep roofs, occupies an exceptional position on the east bank of the Rance; its ramparts survived the destruction of the town in the Second World War.

The attractive town of Dinan stands at the head of the Rance estuary, its old quarter surrounded by ramparts and full of picturesque half-timbered houses. Other Breton towns have likewise preserved and restored their old quarters. Vannes, the ancient and important historic capital in the Morbihan gulf, is a delightful town whose medieval houses are grouped around the cathedral of St-Pierre.

Quimper, famous for its pottery, Gothic cathedral and folklore festival, is one example of the extraordinary wealth of Breton towns; Vitré, Morlaix, St-Brieuc and Lannion are others. The Place de l'Église in the centre of Locronan, which once flourished on the manufacture of sailcloth, is a beautiful little square with an old well and fine granite houses. Concarneau, an important fishing port where the Filets Bleus (blue nets) festival is held annually, has a famous Ville Close (walled town) surrounded by massive granite ramparts.

Many fortresses testify to the power struggle between rival claimants to the Duchy when there was scarcely a let-up in sieges and attacks. The castles at Fougères and Vitré are amongst the finest in France; the towers of Dinan and

(OPPOSITE) Wandering through the old quarters and looking at timber-framed houses are some of the pleasures of a visit to Brittany. The Rue de Jerzual is typical of the centre of Dinan.

(ABOVE) The Place des Lices, Rennes, once the scene of jousting and tournaments.

(TOP) Fifteenth- and sixteenth-century wooden houses in St-Brieuc.

(ABOVE) The Château de Vitré, proudly sited on the top of a rocky spur, was rebuilt several times between the thirteenth and fifteenth centuries.

(OPPOSITE) Château de la Bretesche, with its beautiful lake bordered by forest, Missillac (Loire-Atlantique).

Combourg still stand proudly above their towns; the remote ruins of Suscinio, La Hunaudaye and Tonquédec provide marvellous examples of military architecture; and the impressive fortifications of Kerjean and Josselin conceal interiors of palatially furnished apartments.

Scattered across the countryside are the fortified manor houses, some with watchtowers, that testify to Brittany's defensive past. There are many in Léon, including Kergroadès, Kérouzéré, Kergornadeac'h and Traonjoly. Castles of a later date, such as Rocher-Portail and Lanrigan, no longer have the appearance of fortification; their sobriety and simplicity suggest more prosperous times. Other castles – La Bourbansais, Bonne-Fontaine, Caradeuc and Rosanbo – have marvellous surroundings, with gardens and parkland.

Artistic inspiration

UNDER limpid skies with a melancholy succession of rain and storm, Brittany's harsh landscape, rugged coastline and busy ports – as well as the strong local traditions – have attracted a succession of painters, from the illustrious Turner, who visited Brittany in 1826, to artists of today.

Whether drawn by the fascination of a particular place, the inspiration of a painter or the friendliness of a small country inn, artists have tended to group together, forming colonies that flourished sometimes for months and often for years. Douarnenez, Concarneau and Pont-Aven in the Cornouaille district, followed by Quimper and Le Pouldu, have been the most favoured locations, although the Guérande peninsula, Camaret, Le Faou and Belle-Île have also at times been popular.

During their time in Brittany, many artists produced work that has been influential in changing the course of art history. The decisive paintings of Eugène Boudin, for instance, in Le Faou, Camaret and Plougastel, were to herald the revolution of Impressionism.

Similarly, the charm of the small Breton village of Pont-Aven captivated many an artist who gathered round Paul Gauguin in the 1880s to invent new forms of artistic expression. The Pont-Aven School consisted of some twenty painters, including Gauguin himself, Émile Bernard, Paul Sérusier, Lacombe and others. In rejecting the Impressionist and Pointillist movements, these artists worked from memory and towards simplification of form and elimination of detail in a palette of strong, flat colours. Their strongly symbolist art, which became known as Synthetism,

was eventually to pave the way for the Nabis, a group taking their name from the Hebrew word for prophet.

Corot, Monet, Renoir, Vuillard, Matisse, Marquet, Derain and Delaunay also spent time developing their art and techniques in Brittany.

The Breton character

Populated by Celtic settlers from Cornwall in the fifth century BC, Brittany, like other Celtic lands fringing the Atlantic, has kept alive many of its ancient myths and associations. In the Léon, Trégorrois, Cornouaille and Vannetais districts, deep-rooted customs and traditional costumes, language and culture give Brittany an identity that is quite distinct from that of the rest of France.

Adventurous in spirit, like the modern single-handed Breton sailors who have pitted themselves against the elements to prove their will to succeed, the people of Brittany have always been hard-working, opinionated, proud and stubborn. Whether on land or at sea, they have shown a courageous and indomitable character that is also found at the heart of the Breton family.

Alongside its continuing popularity as a place for holidays, Brittany has fiercely preserved its identity and the Breton people their sense of hospitality.

(OPPOSITE) Gauguin's Bretonnes *have become as well known as his paintings of the Breton countryside.*

(LEFT) Le lavoir à St-Nicolas-du-Pélem, *by Stanislava de Karlowska. Scenes of traditional Breton domestic life, as in the laundry where the women used to do their washing on their knees, were an inspiration for a number of painters.*

(RIGHT) Femmes bretonnes aux ombrelles, *by Émile Bernard.*

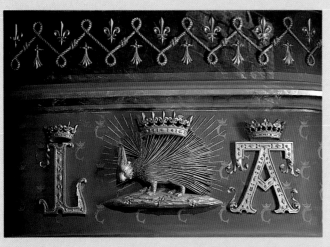

The Loire Valley

The quiet charm of the Loire Valley, perhaps the most characteristic of all the regions of France. The river flows through the Orléanais, Touraine and Anjou départements in turn.

A traveller hurriedly passing through the Loire Valley on one or other of its great highways might be forgiven for dismissing the countryside, with its low hills and unrelieved stretches of moors and forests, as rather uninteresting and ordinary. It is the valleys, however, that give the Loire region its physical characteristics and justify its opulent reputation. Here the exceptionally fertile alluvial soil, known as *varenne*, yields in abundance the much-prized early fruit and vegetables, in particular asparagus. Bordering the valleys are the limestone hillsides that produce the region's famous wines.

At the first hint of spring the fruit trees blossom in a symphony of colour that lights up the horizon. Under skies flecked with rapidly moving storm clouds the dappled light streams on to the slate roofs of sleepy white tufa villages, completely transforming them.

To savour the real beauty of this countryside – as celebrated by the great French writers Ronsard, Balzac and Alfred de Vigny – you should take the smaller roads that cut across the region, find the source of the Loire, follow its tributaries and get in step with the rhythm of this royal river.

It is only by meandering along the banks of the Loire that one can appreciate the subtle beauty of its leisurely flow. From one hour to the next the play of light, which inspired Turner to paint his *Views of the Loire*, constantly changes; every now and again clear sunlight bathes the scene with a softness that is almost Italian. As the French historian Hippolyte Taine wrote in 1895: 'the Loire flows slowly, with a wide, almost immobile motion, and one's spirit sweeps along at the same pace.'

(ABOVE) *Rising out of a green foreground, the church of St-Florent-le-Vieil on top of a rocky headland.*

(LEFT) *Hunting at Cheverny.*

(OPPOSITE) *Château d'Azay-le-Rideau, built from 1518 to 1529, reflected in the calm waters of the Indre.*

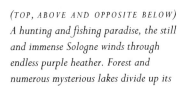

(TOP, ABOVE AND OPPOSITE BELOW) A hunting and fishing paradise, the still and immense Sologne winds through endless purple heather. Forest and numerous mysterious lakes divide up its territory. The river stretches right up to towns and villages where brick, stone and wood add a colourful note to the traditional houses.

(TOP RIGHT AND RIGHT) Bordered by a beautiful forest and dominated by the ruins of the castle, the pointed roofs and tortuous streets of old Chinon.

The garden of France

AROUND Orléans the valley opens out into a richly horticultural area of nurseries specializing in seedlings and rosebushes. Downstream, the Loire winds between the wheat fields of the Petit Beauce and the flat countryside of the Sologne, where the woodlands abound in game and the ponds in fish. Bordering the Sologne is the mysterious *bocage* farmland described in Alain Fournier's novel, *Le Grand Meaulnes*. As the Loire flows through Touraine and Anjou the climate becomes milder. Mulberry trees, introduced in the reign of Louis XI and the source of the raw material for the silk-makers of Tours, palm and fig trees flourish on the river banks.

Where the Loire has worn its course through the soft tufa chalk it has hollowed caves used for wine cellars and curious habitations in the cliffs. Islands lie dotted along the river, sheltered by peaceful clumps of trees. The hillsides are covered in vines which have made the names Montlouis, Vouvray, Bourgueil, Anjou and Saumur famous.

Past Angers, the Loire flows through green wooded farmland divided by hedges and criss-crossed by sunken lanes. It runs alongside the schist country of Anjou Noir, then on to the Segréen region, where slate is quarried, bordered by the Pays des Mauges to the south.

Rivers and valleys

THE tributaries of the Loire have been the inspiration for writers and poets as well as for the architects who built the great Renaissance châteaux that line the river banks. The Indre, the setting for Balzac's novel *Lys dans la Vallée*, idles between green banks to wash round the slender outline of Azay-le-Rideau. Before merging into the Loire at Avoine, it reflects the myriad turrets of the Château d'Ussé, supposedly the model for Sleeping Beauty's fairy-tale castle.

The Cher flows unobtrusively through meadows until it reaches Chenonceau. Here it is bridged by the beautiful sixteenth-century castle in a perfect harmony of water, gardens, park and trees. Before joining the Vienne in Touraine, the little-known Creuse wanders through hilly, picturesque countryside sprinkled with castles and villages. The fertile Vienne valley is dotted with marvellous Romanesque churches which show the influence of Poitou. The crypt in the church at Tavant, on the south bank of the Vienne, has some remarkable twelfth-century frescoes.

The fish-filled waters of the Loir wind placidly through the gentle countryside of 'La Douce France', the birthplace of the poet Ronsard. In the Middle Ages, pilgrims on the road to Santiago followed the upper reaches of the river before turning south to Tours; many churches and priories were built along the way. At Angers the waters of the Maine are joined by those of the Loir, Sarthe and the Mayenne. The quiet Mayenne is ideal for river cruises and boating; in its upper reaches, it flows through wild countryside between steep wooded banks.

(ABOVE) Dominating the Indre and set against the backdrop of the forest of Chinon, the Château d'Ussé stands above its beautiful terraced gardens. Its imposing size and fortified towers are relieved by the white stone in which it is built. The castle's extraordinary roofscape bristles with pinnacles, dormers and chimneys.

(OPPOSITE) Pastoral scene in the Loire Valley, strongly reminiscent of an eighteenth-century English painted landscape.

(ABOVE) The ancient Place Plumereau, Tours; surrounded by handsome fifteenth-century houses with alternating wood and stone façades.

(RIGHT) Fountain, Le Mans.

(FAR RIGHT) The towers of Orléans Cathedral, with the Pont George V, the ancient royal bridge, in the foreground.

(OPPOSITE) In the old archbishopric of Tours, the round tower from the remains of the Gallo-Roman wall and the southern tower of the cathedral.

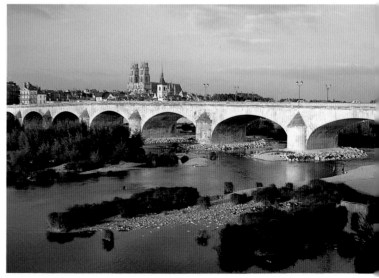

Trade and the Loire

IN the first few centuries AD, the Loire brought life to the region by transporting goods such as luxurious ceramic tableware, wine and marble from Italy, as well as porphyry from Asia. Seafood and oysters were shipped upstream from Nantes to Tours, while local produce, notably wine, was exported. In the sixth century, there is evidence of Greek, Syrian and Jewish traders in Orléans.

The Viking invaders took advantage of the navigability of the river, and in the ninth century sailed up as far as St-Benoît-sur-Loire, ravaging the towns as they passed. After a while local trade picked up again; merchants banded together in guilds and, braving the sandbanks and floods, rapidly developed the river traffic. In the seventeenth and eighteenth centuries Orléans became an enormous port with warehousing.

Travellers also used the waterway, loading their carriages on to rafts, as did Madame de Sévigné when she made her journey to Brittany.

The building of abbeys and castles depended on the Loire and its tributaries for the transportation of the stone. The quarries of the Cher, for instance, supplied the stone for the enormous Château de Chambord, but water levels fluctuated and when the river ran dry in the summer of 1539 the builders ran out of stone.

Up to the mid-nineteenth century, the Loire was plied by the flat-bottomed boats with white sails seen in contemporary engravings. Here and there, in the churches attached to former sailing communities, a model boat offered in thanksgiving commemorates the vitality of these boatmen's guilds.

THE great pilgrimages of the early Middle Ages converged on the banks of the Loire, at the burial places of St Martin and St Benedict.

In Tours, the monumental bronze statue on the dome of the basilica representing St Martin as bishop, and the two towers of the cathedral of St Gatien, stand like sentinels above the city. Inside the cathedral, the famous stained-glass windows in the chancel trace the life of St Martin in two sets of coloured medallions. Over the centuries the shrine of St Martin has attracted many pilgrims, including kings of France as well as the poor and suffering, and numerous miracles are believed to have taken place through the intercession of the healing saint. The relics of St Martin are contained in the crypt of the neo-Byzantine-style church built at the turn of the century by Victor Laloux, the designer of the Gare d'Orsay in Paris. The remains of the huge medieval basilica are dotted about the streets near the new basilica; they include the Tour de Charlemagne, the Tour de l'Horloge (clock tower) and the Musée St-Martin.

Some distance upstream, the relics of St Benedict are contained in the monastery of Fleury in St-Benoît-sur-Loire, one of the earliest centres of intellectual life in the West. In the tenth century the renown of the abbey's monastic school had reached as far as England. The basilica's richly carved capitals were long regarded as an inexhaustible source of inspiration for sculptors of the Romanesque style throughout the region. Not far from here stands the precious church of Germigny-des-Prés, a rare example of Carolingian art built by the brilliant scholar Theodulf, adviser to Charlemagne.

The Abbaye de Fontevraud, on the borders of Anjou and Touraine, consists of a group of monastic buildings almost as large as a town. It was founded by Robert d'Arbrissel, who took the unusual step of appointing an abbess to take sole charge of the three men's and two women's priories. The chancel of the Romanesque abbey church is reached through a sombre nave roofed by a series of domes; the increasing light is symbolic, signifying the Christian aspiration of the ascent to heaven. Members of the Plantagenet royal family, who heaped wealth on the abbey, lie buried in the crypt. In many ways the Plantagenets considered themselves to be more Angevin than English and chose the abbey as their last resting place. Among them are Henry II, his wife Eleanor of Aquitaine and their son Richard Coeur-de-Lion. These recumbent figures are interesting examples of funerary Gothic sculpture.

(OPPOSITE) The power and serenity of the Romanesque Notre-Dame church, at Beaugency.

(ABOVE) The façade of St-Gatien Cathedral, Tours.

(RIGHT) A rare and precious example of Carolingian art, the little church of Germigny-des-Prés is one of the oldest in France. Detail of the mosaic on the vault of the east apse.

A land of princes

DETAIL, LANGEAIS.

A̲T the turn of the eleventh century, the counts of Anjou fought the counts of Blois, who also held Champagne, for supremacy over the Loire region. Fulk Nerra, the most famous conquering warlord of the Angevin dynasty, combined acts of treachery and cruelty with sudden fits of Christian repentance. As a result of this feudal rivalry, the land between Château-Gontier and Montrichard bristles with defensive keeps, some still proud and haughty as at Montbazon, others, like Langeais, truncated and weathered by the assault of years.

In the twelfth century the Angevin dynasty reached the height of its power under the Plantagenets. When Henri, Count of Anjou, ascended the throne of England as Henry II, a fifty-year period of war with the Capetian monarchy began. In 1205 Anjou and Touraine were won back for the French crown. The building of the monumental castle at Angers, with its black and white striped towers, sealed the return of the Capetian sphere of influence.

The handsome town of Chinon, with its narrow winding streets, is situated on the banks of the Vienne river and crowned by the imposing ruins of its medieval fortress. It was here, in 1429, that Joan of Arc, the shepherdess from Domrémy, arrived from Lorraine to see the dauphin, the future Charles VII. The message she conveyed to him was eventually to rid France of the English and to alter the course of history.

Along the banks of the Loire between Gien and Angers is a ribbon of fortresses, abbeys and palaces rich in historical associations. Among the royal châteaux are the sober red-brick Gien; Sully-sur-Loire, where Joan of Arc persuaded the French king to be crowed at Reims; Loches, where Agnès Sorel, Charles VII's mistress, took refuge; Amboise, luxuriously decorated by Charles VIII and the childhood home of the future François I; and Saumur, now the home of the crack Cadre Noir cavalry squad. The basilica of Notre-Dame-de-Cléry contains the royal vault of Louis XI. This monarch built the austere château at Langeais, where later Charles VIII married Anne of Brittany.

Statue of Joan of Arc, Orléans.

(LEFT) The important fortress of
Sully-sur-Loire.

(TOP) Angers, the stronghold built by
St Louis.

(ABOVE) Massive and elegant, Château
de Saumur stands alone above the town.

Cradle of the French Renaissance

CHAMBORD'S
ROOFSCAPE OF CHIMNEYS, STAIRCASES
AND DORMER WINDOWS.

A T the Château d'Amboise, the silhouette of pointed towers and rooftops seems to spring out of its very ramparts. It was here, on Charles VIII's return from Italy in 1495, that a new artistic style was born. The king brought back with him teams of artists, architects and decorators as well as fabrics and works of art. The result was a successful blending of Italian refinement and French tradition that breathed new life into the art of building and luxurious living. Many of the monumental buildings in the Loire Valley bear the stamp of the Renaissance: Châteaudun, Blois, Loches, Le Lude, Valençay and Azay-le-Rideau, where the straight-ramped staircase replaced the Gothic spiral. At Villandry, clipped box hedges form a complex symbolic design outlining the flower beds and ornamental kitchen gardens.

Described by the romantic poet Alfred de Vigny as 'a brilliant daydream which suddenly materialized', Chambord was built to the orders of François I with a total of 440 rooms and 365 fireplaces. The genius of Leonardo da Vinci, installed as the king's guest at Le Clos-Lucé in Amboise, hovers over it. He may have designed the famous central staircase, a double spiral of marvellous architectural ingenuity. The staircase leads up to the roof terrace where the sentry path winds through a maze of lanterns, chimneys, stairs and dormer windows.

(LEFT) A view into one of the lantern turrets, Chambord.

(ABOVE) The first of France's great classical palaces, Chambord stands in a vast park enclosed by a 32-kilometre wall beyond which stretches the forest of Sologne.
At the age of twenty-one, François I had just returned in triumph from his

victory over the Swiss at Marignano, which had given him possession of the duchy of Milan. Dissatisfied with the old residence at Blois, in spite of the improvements he had made, he had a vision of a dream castle to be built some distance away on the forest's edge. Leonardo da Vinci may have helped with the plans for this fabulous building: its central keep and corner towers disguise its purpose as a palace of pleasure and status symbol for a Renaissance prince. Begun in 1519, Chambord was also worked on by Philibert Delorme, Jean Bullant and Mansart.

At Azay-le-Rideau and Chenonceau the financial advisers to the kings vied with their princes in a display of luxury that earned them bitter disgrace and confiscation of their property. Chenonceau housed the royal mistresses: on the death of Henri II, his widow Catherine de' Medici, having dislodged the king's lover Diane de Poitiers, gave dazzling parties there.

More attached to their homeland than to the glamour of court life, the sixteenth-century poets du Bellay, native of Anjou, and Ronsard, from Vendôme, dedicated themselves to their poetry in the Loire Valley, where they formed the literary circle of the Renaissance Pléiade.

In the following century, the canons of classicism were brought to perfection at the Château de Cheverny, which has a rare unity of style in both its decoration and its architecture. A similarly ambitious example of classical urban planning is the town of Richelieu, built by the cardinal of the same name.

(LEFT) Early seventeenth-century French ceiling in the Château de Cheverny. Built between 1604 and 1634, the castle is a perfect example of severe classical architecture. The apartments, reached by a magnificent Louis XIII staircase, contain a wealth of furniture from the seventeenth to nineteenth centuries.

(ABOVE) Azay-le-Rideau. The architecture belongs to the French Gothic tradition of the fifteenth century but its defences, cornice, pepperpot towers and turrets are purely decorative.

(ABOVE AND RIGHT) Villandry. The castle was rebuilt from 1536, on ancient foundations, for Jean le Breton, ambassador to Italy. In the potager garden, 85,000 flower and vegetable plants are divided into compartments by clipped box. The cultivation of even the simplest produce, such as cabbage and cauliflower, can become an art when chosen for their culinary value, symbolism, therapeutic qualities or colours.

(BELOW RIGHT) The gardens of Azay-le-Rideau.

(OPPOSITE, TOP AND BOTTOM) The great Renaissance Château de Chenonceau was built from 1513 to 1521 for Thomas Bohier, financial adviser to François I. The rectangular building has corner turrets and oeils-de-boeuf dormer windows decorated with cherubs. Six women were mistress of this castle, three of whom — Catherine Briçonnet, Diane de Poitiers and Catherine de' Medici — marked it with their personalities.

A gentle way of life

DELICATE RIPENING
OF A BOTTLED PEAR.

THE Loire Valley is enchanting in springtime. While the grey of winter still lingers in the countryside around the Île-de-France, climbing roses bloom in the villages along the Loire; soon after comes the season for country hollyhocks and delicate clusters of wisteria.

At the priory of St Cosmas, Ronsard took great satisfaction in the simple pleasures of caring for his vegetables – artichokes, lettuces, asparagus and parsnips, as well as pumpkins that had recently been introduced into Touraine by Charles VIII. Today, asparagus from the Blois region, potatoes from Saumur, Reinette apples from Le Mans, French beans from Touraine and artichokes from Angers all ripen before those in the Paris region, and are therefore highly prized in the capital.

The waters of the Loire and Loir are full of fish, particularly pike and shad. Eels, which are caught on their way down to the sea to spawn, are a feature in local restaurants. In a countryside devoted to hunting, shooting and good living, farmers fatten up pigs for the annual slaughter when storerooms fill up with *rillettes* and other traditional potted pork meats. Even the poorer land on the plateau around

Ste-Maure-de-Touraine has a high yield of produce, notably fresh, creamy goat cheeses.

Local wine is stored in former stone quarries hewn out of limestone slopes. These cellars, to which the faithful flock as though on a pilgrimage, are the best places for the visitor to appreciate the character of the region. Here, after showing his visitors round the bottle-filled vaults, the wine-grower typically presides over the ceremonial tasting: full-bodied Sancerre; dry, mellow Vouvray; heady Montlouis; Chinon with its aftertaste of violets; Bourgueil with its hint of raspberries or wild strawberries; the Angevin wines such as sparkling Saumur and the dry white Saumur; and wines from La Coulée du Serrant and the Layon.

In the Loire Valley the traditions of good living and the cultural heritage coexist with the latest technology of the modern world: the sophisticated motorway network around Tours, the controversial and impressive nuclear power stations at St-Laurent-des-Eaux and Chinon, and the Atlantic line for France's high-speed train. In June, the world's most famous endurance test for cars, the twenty-four-hour race at Le Mans, takes place just south of the city.

Several famous fourteenth-century tapestries from the Loire workshops survive in museums in Saumur, Langeais and Angers. The work that perhaps best epitomizes the Loire Valley today, however, is Jean Lurçat's masterpiece, the *Chant du Monde* (song of the world). This tapestry, 80 metres long and begun in 1957, is exhibited at Angers. Inspired by the Apocalypse, it evokes man's universal joys and agonies in an extraordinary synthesis of shapes, colours and rhythms.

(LEFT) Vineyard in the Loire Valley. The best way of getting to know the region is to visit its wine cellars. This cellar, once an old quarry, opens into the white chalk hillside on the level of the road; its vaults stretch for several hundred metres. Some of the larger 'rooms' are used for all sorts of local festivities, reunions and banquets.

(OPPOSITE) The Loire Valley, the garden of France.

Paris and the Île-de-France

*Its light, architecture and special atmosphere
make Paris a city of dreams and discoveries.
Its prestige is enhanced by its rich setting
amongst forests, castles and cathedrals.*

In the beginning was the Seine

MENTION the capital of France and any number of images spring to mind: the broad sweep of the Champs-Élysées, the elegant palaces housing world-famous museums, the glorious stained glass windows of Notre-Dame Cathedral, the narrow streets of the Latin Quarter, the bridges over the river Seine, the bustling street cafés and, not least, the Tour d'Eiffel etched against the skyline. As its inhabitants go about their daily business in this great, sprawling city, millions of others, visitors from France and abroad, succumb to its atmosphere and charms every year.

Flowing through the heart of Paris, like a main artery, is the river Seine. This graceful river, which has shaped the capital's history and provided its motto *fluctuat nec mergitur* ('though buffeted by the waves she does not sink'), provides the key to understanding and discovering the city. Its generous sweeps form the familiar silhouette of the capital and make its layout so memorable.

Taking its course between the hills of Buttes-Chaumont, Montmartre and Chaillot to the north and the Montagne Ste-Geneviève to the south, the river Seine has also played its part in shaping the softly undulating relief of the region. The symbolic man-made landmarks of the Sacré-Coeur basilica on Montmartre and the Panthéon on the Montagne Ste-Geneviève now crown these natural outcrops, disguising their gentle slopes.

(TOP) *Strange and poetic atmosphere of Paris by night.*

(LEFT) *Morning light on the Seine.*

(OPPOSITE) *The Pont Neuf wrapped by the artists Christo and Jeanne-Claude.*

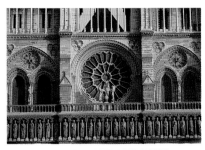

THE GREAT ROSE WINDOW, NOTRE-
DAME CATHEDRAL.

Anchored in a meander of the river, the now-famous Île de la Cité saw the installment, in the third century BC, of the first settlers, the Parisii, from whom the city takes its name.

Frankish and early Capetian monarchs built castles here and in the twelfth century Bishop Maurice de Sully began the construction of the magnificent cathedral of Notre-Dame. Sainte-Chapelle, an outstanding example of High Gothic architecture, was built by Louis IX (St Louis) to house the relics of the Passion; it was consecrated in 1248. In the reigns of Philippe-Auguste, Charles V and Louis XIII successive rings of fortifications were erected, principally to guard against the threat of attack and protect the city's overspill. As new abbeys and convents were founded, new land reclaimed and cultivated, and new branches of trade and industry developed along the city's excellent communication routes the city walls expanded. By the eighteenth century the royal family were ensconced in luxurious apartments at the palace of Versailles, and a new fortified city wall was built around Paris by Ledoux.

All over the city evidence can be found of the historical evolution of Parisian architecture up to the French Revolution: the tiny medieval streets of the Latin quarter around the beautiful old churches of St-Séverin and St-Julien-le-Pauvre; the elegant Renaissance and classical mansions of the Marais; the Palais du Louvre, the symbol of royal power; l'Institut de France, built by Le Vau; Place Vendôme, the model for all France's most beautiful squares; the magnificent classical architecture of Les Invalides, dominated by the gilded dome of its Louis XIV church; and the Place de la Concorde, the embodiment of Louis XV style.

Paris is a city of contrasts, and never fails to provoke a response from those who visit it. Thus, at the very heart of the Louvre in the Cour Napoléon, surrounded by the extravagantly decorated façades of Napoleon III's palace, stands the uncompromisingly geometric creation of I. M. Pei's steel and glass pyramid which forms the museum's main entrance. The elegant old Marais district has as its next-door neighbour the squat bulk of the Centre Georges-Pompidou. This building, swathed in brightly coloured tubes and steel framework, is the work of the Anglo-Italian partnership of Rogers and Piano. The fine Renaissance decoration of the church of St-Eustache forms a backdrop to the white-framed glass arcades of the neighbouring Forum des Halles. It is architectural juxtapositions like these that make Paris such an exciting city to visit today.

(LEFT) The arcades of the Place des Vosges, in the heart of the Marais — a perfect place for a stroll.

(OPPOSITE TOP) Sainte-Chapelle, the upstairs chapel. The dazzling sight of the stained glass windows, which capture the slightest ray of sunlight, is one of the most moving experiences in Paris .

(OPPOSITE BOTTOM) Cour Napoléon, Louvre. Time telescoped between the majestic façades of the old palace and the geometric lines of I.M.Pei's famous pyramid, which serves as the entrance to one of the world's greatest museums.

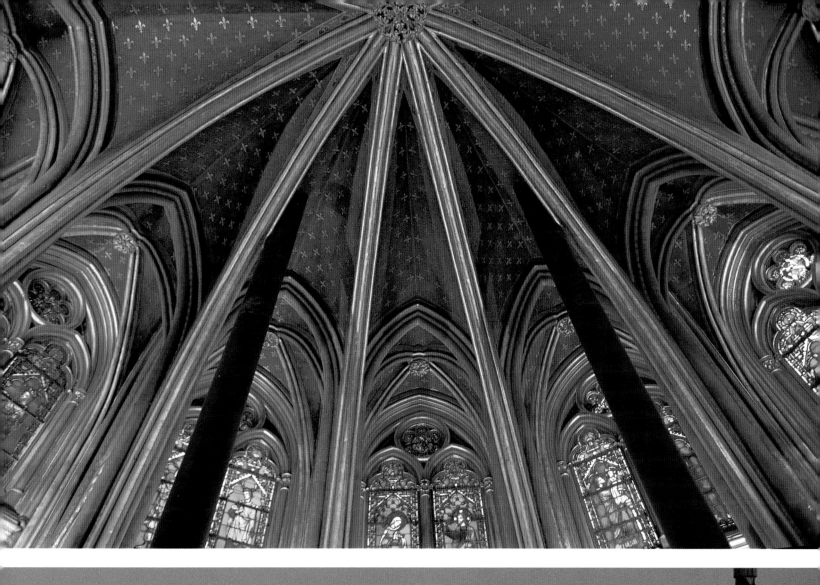

A royal land

EMBLEM OF THE SUN-KING.

PARIS lies at the heart of rolling green countryside, with rivers, valleys and magnificent forests such as those at Fontainebleau and Rambouillet, which rank among the most beautiful in France. For centuries, the game forests not only were a source of food but also provided the royal court with sport. Today they are a haven for Parisians and others looking for an antidote to urban life.

The privileged position of the region – the wealth of its natural resources coupled with its proximity to the seat of political power – has left it an exceptional legacy of fine buildings. Châteaux and stately country houses, masterpieces of Renaissance and classical architecture, were built around lavish parks and formal gardens created by the leading landscape gardeners of the age.

The palace of Versailles is a memorial to the French monarchy at the height of its powers. Constructed for Louis XIV, the Sun King, over several decades, the architectural ensemble was the work of Le Vau followed by Mansart, with interiors by Le Brun. Besides the main palace there are two smaller palaces, the Grand and Petit Trianons; together they represent the pinnacle of French classicism. The extensive gardens and parkland were designed by Le Nôtre.

Influenced by his campaigns in Italy, François I introduced Italian Renaissance ideas to the court at Fontainebleau. He brought in an army of gifted artists, among whom were Rosso and Primaticcio, who worked on the decoration of the palace in fresco, stucco and other materials, producing wonderful masterpieces of art.

The elegant Château de Chantilly, which houses superb collections of manuscripts, drawings and paintings, is set in a beautiful park on the edge of a forest. In the grounds are the fine eighteenth-century stables, a horse and pony museum and the racecourse for which Chantilly is famous.

Amongst the many other châteaux of architectural distinction are Courances, Maisons-Laffitte, Vaux-le-Vicomte, built for Nicolas Fouquet with gardens designed by Le Nôtre, Écouen, Champs, Grosbois, Malmaison, Rambouillet and, in the Chevreuse valley, Dampierre and Breteuil. All have splendid apartments, magnificent collections of furniture and are set in beautiful parkland.

(LEFT) Palais de Fontainebleau, the François 1 gallery. The decoration consists of a mixture of fresco, stucco and panelling.
The palace of Fontainebleau owes its origin to the royal passion for the hunt. Over the years a succession of kings enlarged what was a family residence and decorated it with stunning works of art. Remarkably, the palace was converted and lived in by ruling monarchs from the time of the last Capetian kings to Napoleon III.

(BELOW) Versailles, gardens and fountain of Apollo.
The gardens of Versailles are Le Nôtre's masterpiece. Their great water parterres, fountains and groves of trees provide a balance to the colossal façade of the palace, and give a magnificent view from the royal apartments. Almost two hundred sculptures — statues, decorative vases and busts — adorn these gardens, making Versailles the largest outdoor museum of classical sculpture. Each year the spectacular event of the Grandes Eaux conjures up the heyday of the Ancien Régime.

Chartres Cathedral: the light filtering through the stained glass and the architecture of the nave and choir inspire prayer and meditation.

No other region of France has such wealth of religious buildings. The beautiful churches and abbeys at Senlis, Morienval, St-Leu-d'Esserent, Chaalis, Port-Royal and Royaumont are testaments to deeply held faith.

Soaring above the cornfields of the surrounding countryside, and visible from miles around, is the spire of the magnificent Gothic cathedral at Chartres, the destination of hundreds of pilgrims each year. The inside is lit by the glorious 'Chartres blue' stained-glass windows.

A model for many of the later creations was the basilica of St-Denis, mainly the work of Abbot Suger in the twelfth-century. The innovative design of this church, which houses the remains of twelve centuries of French royalty, marked a turning point in the history of French architecture.

Nineteenth-century grandeur

Iᴛ was under Napoleon III and the man he appointed as his urban planner, Baron Georges-Eugène Haussmann, that Paris was transformed almost beyond recognition.

As part of his ambitious modernization projects, Haussmann razed huge tracts of the old city, little changed since the Middle Ages. Narrow medieval streets, in many cases overcrowded slums, were replaced by straight, elegant boulevards lined with pavements. In his efforts to make the city a worthy capital for his empire, Napoleon I extended the Palais du Louvre, dug out the canals and built triumphal arches at the Louvre Carousel and the Place de l'Étoile. He erected a triumphal column in the Place Vendôme and a mock Greek temple, the church of La Madeleine, to the glory of his army. He also laid out spacious squares, the largest example of which is now known as the Place Charles-de-Gaulle (Étoile); twelve avenues radiate out in a star shape from the Arc de Triomphe, of which the Avenue Foch and the Champs-Élysées are the most prestigious.

Haussmann entrusted Alphand with the laying out of landscaped parks in place of the quarry on the Buttes-Chaumont hill and in the former royal hunting grounds of the Bois de Boulogne and Bois de Vincennes to the west and east of the city. Garnier was the architect responsible for the extravagant Opéra, one of the most remarkable buildings of the Second Empire, as well as for the main railway stations with their bold metal frameworks.

The regular, symmetrical buildings of this period, with their highly decorated stone façades, transformed the face of Paris and reorganized the city. The architectural harmony is still very much in evidence today.

At the same time as Haussmann's *grands boulevards*, numerous covered arcades came to be built, such as the Galeries Vivienne, Colbert, Véro-Dodat and those along the Rue de Rivoli and the Passage Jouffroy. Thanks to their modernity and elegant boutiques, they quickly became the focus of high society. Today, many still exist and, even though some of the former animation and prestige may have been lost, their slightly unusual selection of shops still has an old-fashioned charm.

The world exhibitions held in Paris at the turn of the century stimulated a burst of architectural innovations such as the Grand and Petit Palais. When it was erected for the exhibition of 1889, the Tour d'Eiffel was the tallest building in the world. Though greeted with horror in many quarters at the time, it has since become perhaps the best-known monument in Paris. A masterpiece of lightness, at night it gleams like the work of a silversmith.

(OPPOSITE)The sumptuous crimson and gold interior of the Paris Opéra, its ceiling decorated by Chagall.

(ABOVE) Two examples of 1900s style: the cast-iron dome of the Galeries Lafayette, and an entrance to the Paris métro by Guimard.

Towards the end of the nineteenth century, the 'Belle Époque' ushered in a period of widespread prosperity. Daily life was transformed by technological progress and innovations, such as the opening of the first métro line and of brand-new department stores and restaurants whose décor was inspired by Art Nouveau. The main emphasis of the new artistic style was on flowing asymmetrical lines and stylized vegetal forms. It became, in effect, an official style with a new vocabulary for use in both interior and exterior decorative schemes, as well as in ceramics and glass. Guimard was the most famous exponent of Art Nouveau style, particularly in his wrought-iron entrances for the newly opened métro.

At the end of the eighteenth century the Avenue des Champs-Élysées had been little more than a muddy field. Now it became a focal point for fashionable society, with elegant town houses, fountains and pavements lit by gas lamps. Chic cafés and restaurants sprung up in the shape of Laurent, Le Fouquet, Ledoyen and, notably, Maxim's, which opened in the Rue Royale in 1893 and whose Art Nouveau decoration provided a place for a sophisticated and sometimes eccentric clientele to see and be seen.

Along these grand boulevards paraded elegant ladies on the arms of men dressed in the height of fashion. Theatre, opera and *cafés-concerts* drew the crowds, and on race days at Longchamp and during the world exhibitions the numbers would swell. Artists, writers, entertainers, political figures, entrepreneurs – anybody who was anybody – flocked to the capital to join the great social whirl, known at the time as 'le Tout-Paris'.

'Belle Époque' Paris: ironwork of the Gare d'Orsay, and Art Nouveau in the Avenue Rapp and the restaurant Fermette Marbeuf.

Twentieth-century Paris

BRASSERIE LE DÔME

AT the turn of the century the artistic and literary life of the capital was centred on Montmartre, to which artists and men of letters were attracted by the picturesque life on the Butte. Later it moved to Montparnasse and St-Germain-des-Prés.

Montmartre, with its steep streets and steps, green spaces and vines, was still a village. Here, Bohemian poets and painters sought inspiration away from the bustle of the busy boulevards, and artists and writers would gather for evening cabarets in the Lapin Agile café or meet in the the Bateau-Lavoir studios, the high spot of painting and modern poetry where Picasso, Braque and Juan Gris invented Cubism. At the Moulin Rouge, founded in 1889, they came to watch performers such as Yvette Guilbert, Jane Avril and Louise Weber, the 'Goulue', whose talents were immortalized on canvas by Toulouse-Lautrec.

Gradually, as Montmartre gave itself up to nightlife, the focus of artistic society shifted to the Left Bank at Montparnasse. Still a country town until the villages of Plaisance, Vaugirard and Montrouge were joined to Paris, Montparnasse was the fashionable district in the inter-war years. Poets and writers, many of them foreign – for example, F. Scott Fitzgerald, Ezra Pound, T. S. Eliot and James Joyce – installed themselves here. La Ruche succeeded the Bateau-Lavoir studios and provided lodgings and studios for Modigliani, Chagall, Soutine and other painters of the Paris School, as well as for the Surrealist Salvador Dalí.

The brasseries that opened along the Boulevard Montparnasse were a meeting-place for political exiles from Russia (notably Lenin and Trotsky), musicians, poets and painters. Next to the Observatory in the Latin Quarter, La Closerie des Lilas was the venue for dazzling evenings. Today, Montparnasse still attracts a lively crowd, and, even if its restaurants and bars have lost much of their authenticity and no longer have their original décor, it is impossible not to feel the tug of nostalgia when entering their doors.

In the first half of the twentieth century St-Germain-des-Prés, a relative backwater up until the First World War, became the melting-pot for radical intellectual ideas. Rarely has a district of Paris made such an impact on the art and thinking of a whole generation. Its cafés, the salons of the literary avant-garde, attracted writers, poets and philosophers such as Apollinaire, André Breton, Jean-Paul Sartre and Simone de Beauvoir, who could be found deep in discussion at all hours of the day in the Cafés de Flore and des Deux Magots and the Brasserie Lipp, where later Ernest Hemingway wrote most of *A Farewell to Arms*.

Following the liberation of Paris, basement jazz clubs and cabarets swung to the sound of Duke Ellington and his New Orleans contemporaries, a musical revolution mirroring that taking place in art and philosophy. This was the age of existentialism and the philosophy of the absurd.

(*OPPOSITE*) *The view from the top of the Butte Montmartre looks out over the whole of Paris.*

(*ABOVE*) *In St-Germain-des-Prés, the Cafés de Flore and des Deux Magots are famous as the meeting places of Left Bank artists and intellectuals.*

The important architectural achievements of this period brought the city considerable prestige. For the 1937 exhibition, the Chaillot hill was adorned with two neo-classical palaces, the Palais de Chaillot, a spectacular low semi-circle of white stone, and the Palais de Tokyo. After the Second World War, under the influence of Le Corbusier, the aesthetics of architecture underwent a complete transformation. The result was a variety of styles seen in the circular Maison de Radio France, in the Y-shaped UNESCO building, supported on *pilotis*, and in the CNIT building at La Défense, with its sweeping concrete vault poised on its triangular points of support.

In recent years, glass façades – the high-rise office blocks of La Défense, the Arab World Institute and the Cartier Foundation for Contemporary Art – and technically complex concrete constructions – the Palais des Congrès, the Montparnasse tower and the Grande Arche at La Défense –

have also contributed to the changing face of Paris. With space at a premium, many architectural projects have involved the redevelopment of entire districts, as at Maine-Montparnasse, Les Halles and La Villette, or the creation of completely new areas, as at La Défense and surrounding the new Bibliothèque Nationale de France, currently under construction.

(OPPOSITE) La Géode of La Villette; its external polished steel mirror is as striking as the boldness of the structure housing the cinema.

(TOP LEFT) Reflections of old

buildings in the glass fronts of the Forum des Halles.

(TOP RIGHT) Villa Savoye, Poissy; Le Corbusier's gem of Modernist architecture.

(ABOVE) A team of tightrope walkers on the façade of CNIT, one of the most famous buildings of the La Défense district, before the construction of the Grande Arche.

In its role as capital of the arts, Paris regularly inaugurates new museums, extends existing ones and hosts numerous retrospectives and other exhibitions throughout the city. The Centre Georges-Pompidou houses an exceptional collection of modern and contemporary art; the Musée d'Orsay, created from the old railway station, has a collection of nineteenth- and early twentieth-century art; and the Louvre, a national treasure-house and one of the world's top museums, now displays some of its superb collections of sculpture, paintings and objets d'art in the newly opened Richelieu wing.

Paris not only takes the lead in French intellectual and artistic life, but also is at the centre of economic and international affairs. A byword for high fashion and gastronomy, it has an unrivalled cosmopolitan glamour and sophistication and an enormous range of cultural activities. Whatever the season, there is always something going on, whether it is Bastille Day, celebrated on 14 July, the national Fête de la Musique when, at the summer solstice, every street corner and square are filled with chamber groups, jazz singers and rock musicians, or the Five Nations Rugby Tournament.

(OPPOSITE) Snapshots of Parisian life. From left to right, top and bottom: Passage du Tour de France, Rue de Rivoli; Vénus de Milo among her admirers in the Louvre; Pont Neuf, bedecked in flowers by Kenzo; final touches before a fashion parade at Chanel.

(ABOVE) From left to right, top and bottom: Place de la Bastille at nightfall; a football match near the Tour d'Eiffel; a funfair at the Tuileries; the Arc de Triomphe from the magnificent perspective of the Champs-Élysées.

Paris is always *en fête* – such as when the Pont Neuf is wrapped by the artists Christo and Jeanne-Claude or decorated in mosaics of fresh flowers by the fashion designer Kenzo, when the Avenue des Champs-Élysées is transformed into a glittering scene of fairy lights at Christmas or when the Beaux-Arts carnival takes over the Latin Quarter. Cafés and bistros frequently host live music, every day street entertainers perform impromptu in the piazza of the Centre Georges-Pompidou and even the most ordinary local street market becomes a centre of attraction.

Paris on foot

A LONGSIDE the museums and monuments of the capital's rich heritage is a Paris that is a joy to explore on foot. This everyday Paris, which the entire world envies and which Parisians themselves are glad to discover after a long absence, consists of an alchemy of sounds, sensations and images that make up the life of the capital and form part of each person's sentimental geography. Wandering along the streets, with no particular route in mind and guided by the mood of the moment, is to start on a voyage of discovery.

For tourists and Parisians alike, this is the way to see Paris revealed in all its many facets. Here, the eye might be caught by an ornate wrought-iron balcony, a statue in the middle of a square or a line of blue-grey mansard roofs with *oeil-de-boeuf* windows; there, by a blaze of red geraniums in a window box, or a tiny cobbled courtyard glimpsed through a doorway.

Occasionally, music escaping from who knows where, a plaque on a house recalling some famous resident, such as Voltaire, Victor Hugo and Balzac, a *trompe l'oeil* wall painting,

(LEFT) *The spiral staircase under the pyramid, Musée du Louvre.*

(TOP) *Place des Victoires.*

(ABOVE) *Palais-Royal, a haven of peace in central Paris.*

(OPPOSITE) *Shadows cast by the Tour d'Eiffel, all transparent lightness in spite of the extraordinary network of metallic girders.*

(ABOVE) Chance discoveries along the streets of the capital.
From left to right, and top to bottom: one of the many bookstalls along the Seine; a stylish window under an old fashioned shop sign; an invitation to browse; produce of France; a friendly bistro near St-Sulpice; the dated charm of a toy shop in the Galerie Véro-Dodat.

(OPPOSITE) Relaxing beside the Canal de l'Ourcq, La Villette.

caryatids supporting a balcony, the exotic smell of a spice shop, or simply the flight of pigeons from the middle of a square, arrests the attention. A mime artist perched on a stool, a game of *boules*, the opening of a lock-gate on the St Martin canal or musicians on the banks of the Seine – all these can cause one to stop and watch, revelling in such moments.

Some districts of the capital are better suited than others to the pleasures of walking. The embankments of the Seine, along which the river takes its peaceful course, are a perfect place to begin. Here thousands of booksellers' stalls, whose large green metal boxes open up to display old prints, maps and bargain books, are an invitation to browse away the time. Spanning the Seine are numerous bridges which allow one to walk easily from one bank of the river to another. From them, the views up and down the river are particularly beautiful in the early morning or in the rays of the setting sun. Houseboats, with rows of pot plants on deck, are moored along stretches of the *quais*. Below street level, removed from the noise of the traffic on the expressways, are footpaths along the river itself; in summer these are packed with people soaking up the sun. The *bateaux-mouches*, or tourist boats, which ply up and down the

Seine throughout the day, are an excellent way of seeing central Paris; at night, their powerful floodlights light up majestic façades and throw sculptural detail on bridges into sharp relief.

The Marais is also ideal for exploring on foot. The area between the Centre Georges-Pompidou and the Bastille is a maze of narrow streets punctuated by the occasional old half-timbered house, with its upper storeys corbelled out over the street or wide carriage gateways surmounted by coats of arms. There are magnificent town houses with carved stone façades and intricate wrought-iron balconies. The enchanting seventeenth-century Place des Vosges is the oldest square in Paris. Its thirty-six houses round a central square retain their original symmetrical appearance, with alternate brick and stone facings, steeply pitched grey roofs and dormer windows.

At the heart of the Rive Gauche is the venerable church of St-Germain-des-Prés, the oldest in Paris. The surrounding streets are crammed with bookshops, tiny art galleries and antiques dealers, vestiges of the area's literary and artistic past. At night the streets and cafés buzz to the sound of animated conversation and snatches of music. This is one of the most lively places in Paris.

A number of Parisian gardens are home to small museums. Tucked away in the shade of the paulownias on the charming little Place Fürstemberg, just behind the church of St-Germain-des-Prés, is the Musée Delacroix; south-west of the Trocadéro, the Maison de Balzac is hidden in what might be a country garden; and the Musée Zadkine, just south of the Jardin du Luxembourg, displays some of its sculptures out of doors. Greenery in Paris ranges from tree-lined avenues and tiny patches of grass at the centre of a square, to the expanses of woodland east and west of the city. The Luxembourg and Tuileries gardens illustrate the formal French style of garden design. The Bagatelle, in the Bois de Boulogne, is known for its beautiful rose gardens, and the Albert-Kahn gardens, in the suburb of Boulogne, are divided into different garden styles from various regions of France, as well as from Japan and

China. There are statues in the elegant Parc Monceau (where a number of future presidents of France are said to have been wheeled in their pushchairs) and in the garden of the Musée Rodin. A walk around any of the cemeteries of Paris can be rewarding, whether on the track of famous names, admiring the immense variety of funerary decoration or simply soaking up the peaceful atmosphere along the alleys.

For a bird's-eye picture of the city, there are particularly exhilarating views over the rooftops of Paris from the Montparnasse and Eiffel towers, as well as from Notre-Dame, Sacré-Coeur, the Arc de Triomphe, the Grande Arche at La Défense and the clear-sided escalators and roof-top terrace of the Centre Georges-Pompidou. From whatever perspective you choose, it is impossible to resist the magic of Paris, by day or by night.

(OPPOSITE) *Galeries Lafayette, one of the great Parisian department stores.*

(TOP ROW) *The Luxembourg gardens: a favourite haunt for students from the Latin Quarter and others who come to enjoy its leafy shade, statues, lawns and terraces.*

(BOTTOM ROW) *Recreation in the Tuileries gardens and the Bois de Boulogne.*

The North and East

From Beauvais to Lille and Reims to Strasbourg, the north-east is a region of hard-working, imaginative and cheerful people. Picardy, Flanders, Champagne, Vosges and Alsace have a host of surprises in store.

A watery landscape

THE beauty of the varied countryside of north-east France lies in its rain-washed landscapes and clear streams. Water is the dominant feature of this countryside and the key to understanding it. It is everywhere – not just in the rain and mist, but in the constantly moving sea, the rippling rivers and streams, the disciplined canals and the shimmering surfaces of lakes and marshes.

It is by sea that one enters this region. The gateway is the Côte d'Opale (opal coast), which takes its name from the cream-coloured waves washing against the white sand. Clouds scud across the endless beaches of Le-Touquet-Paris-Plage, adopted by the English in the nineteenth century, and Fort Mahon, where the land yachts skim like dragonflies across the wet sand. Under an ever-changing sky, the English coastline is visible in the distance from the chalk cliffs of Cap Gris-Nez and Cap Blanc-Nez; in the foreground can be seen the fishing trawlers of Boulogne and the harbour cranes of Dunkerque. A few kilometres away, thousands of birds flock to winter on the grassy dunes and salt marshes of the Marquenterre bird sanctuary on the Somme estuary.

On the *blooteland* (bare land) of Flanders, the frontier

between water and land is also fluid. This coastal region, whose land over the years has been gradually rescued from the sea, is dotted with windmills, their great white sails streaking the sky. Inland, the marshes around St-Omer are criss-crossed with *watergangs*, small canals running alongside fields of cauliflower lined with trembling poplars; beside ponds covered with duckweed and water-lilies are the low, whitewashed Flemish farmhouses.

Amiens, in Picardy, is famous for its *hortillonages*, the watery market gardens full of flowers and navigated by noiseless punts. To the east, the rivers Ill and Lauch wash around the timber-framed houses of Petite France, the old tanning and market gardening district of Strasbourg, and of Petite Venise, the picturesque centre of Colmar.

Arrow-straight canals link the coal-mines of the north to the steel mills of Lorraine. Here, the landscape is dominated by electric pylons, blast furnaces and dark pyramids of slag; dazzling white sheets dry in the wind along the precise lines of brick terraced houses and flowers bloom in gardens the size of pocket-handkerchiefs.

Free of such geometrical constraints, the rivers cross plains and valleys, passing through the middle of large towns which come to life on market days. The waters then run into *bocage* countryside, through the woods and pastures of Thiérache and Avesnois where black-and-white Friesian cattle graze, and pass the orchards of Lorraine which rain down showers of golden mirabelle plums.

In the pine forests, vineyards and tobacco plantations of Hohwald in Alsace the rivers divide into a thousand rills and streams before breaking up the mosaic of beet, colza and flax fields of Picardy, Champagne and the Ardennes. The Meuse, the most wily of all rivers, has hollowed out wild gorges and formed regular loops that shelter villages overlooked by peaks such as Les Dames de Meuse and the Mont Malgré Tout.

Abandoning their adventures, the rivers feed into vast lakes on the plains, like Der-Chantecoq and Orient, or in the mountains, like Gérardmer, Lac Noir and Lac Blanc in the Vosges, whose calm and unfathomable depths reflect a sky chased with clouds.

At Vittel and Contrexéville, Plombières and Bains-les-Bains, the thermal springs of Lorraine add a note of sparkling vitality to the scene as those who have come to take the waters stroll, cup in hand, around the bandstands and under the trees.

It is by following the course of the water, along the seashore, across the vast plains, from mineral springs to mountain lakes, that the visitor will discover all the many guises of this marvellous countryside.

(OPPOSITE) A spring at the thermal spa of Contrexéville. Those who come to take the waters are also refreshed by the stimulating climate of this pretty resort.

(ABOVE) The marvellous beach of Le Touquet, which stretches for several miles. At low tide its long, gentle slope of fine, hard sand makes it a perfect place for land-yachting.

(RIGHT) Autumn in the forest of Compiègne, the remains of the immense Forêt de Cuise which once extended from the edge of the Pays de France to the Ardennes.

(OPPOSITE) Champagne vineyard, Bergère-lès-Vertus. From Épernay to Vertus, the Côte des Blancs takes its name from the white grapes planted in its vineyards. Some of its finest wines make prestigious vintages and are used in the blanc de blancs.

(TOP RIGHT) Slag-heaps, Pas-de-Calais. The mining life has not only marked the countryside with its slag-heaps, pit-head beams and miners' cottages, but also has moulded the character of its proud, rugged and independent people.

(CENTRE RIGHT) A roof of beautiful glazed tiles in Colmar.

(BOTTOM RIGHT) Marais Audomarais, Pas-de-Calais. This marsh is the result of patient work undertaken by the monks of St Bertin at St-Omer in the ninth century. The waterways are navigated by traditional flat-bottomed punts.

The battlefield of Europe

STATUE OF JOAN OF ARC, COL DU
BALLON D'ALSACE.

NORTH-EAST France, lying between the Low Countries and Germany, has suffered the repeated devastations of war and invasion.

In the Middle Ages the people saw their land disputed by Flemish counts, German princes and Burgundian dukes and their towns overrun by Spanish and English invaders. To defend themselves they built the strong fortresses and imposing castles that can still be seen at Provins, famous for the red Lancastrian rose, Boulogne, Coucy, Sedan and Haut-Koenigsbourg, whose triple-thick walls on their sandstone spur dominate the Rhenish plain.

Nowadays most are no more than eerie moss-covered ruins, silent witnesses to a time of sieges and sackings, but even today it is impossible to contemplate these buildings without a shudder. Bastions of France, caught in the crossfire of wars, they have seen towns and villages pillaged and burnt to the cries of battle and fires that have turned the night sky blazing red.

More modern times have not spared this region, in spite of the long line of forts running from the northern coast to the Ardennes – 'the Pré Carré' – built by Louis XIV's military architect Vauban to fortify France's frontiers. Neuf-Brisach, a perfect square in the centre of an eight-pointed star, and Bitche, with its pink sandstone ramparts, are both reminders of this era when the art of war was compatible with formal architectural beauty.

In 1870 the French were defeated by Prussian forces at Sedan, after which Alsace and much of Lorraine were ceded to Germany. The World Wars of 1914-18 and 1939-45 saw hundreds of thousands of men enter battle, many of whom lie buried under the forests of white crosses in the cemeteries of Verdun and Notre-Dame-de-Lorette. The trenches and shell craters of Verdun, the blockhouse of Eperlecques and the galleries of the Simserhof (the largest underground complex of the Maginot Line) are each moving memorials to the immense cost in human life of the barbaric conflicts of the twentieth century.

Resilience and solidarity in the face of invasions and the enemy are the characteristics of the people of northern France. Their spirit is echoed in the church belfries, whose bells ring out their pride and freedom across the roofs and gables of Douai, Maubeuge and Dunkerque, in the spires of the great cathedrals of Picardy, Champagne, Alsace and Lorraine, and in the high mountains of the Vosges.

For all their independence of mind and spirit, the people are hospitable and welcoming. This land – close to Belgium, the Netherlands and Germany and separated from Britain by only a few miles of water – has a feel of the old Continent as well as of the new Europe, whose capital Strasbourg is the symbol of supra-national politics.

(OPPOSITE) The British military cemetery of Hermonville, in the Marne: a moving memorial of the Great War.

(BELOW) The Burghers of Calais, sculpture by Rodin (1895), Calais.

(BELOW RIGHT) Gravelines, protected behind Vauban's seventeenth-century fortifications.

Art and Culture

PAINTED FAÇADE OF THE MAISON
CHRISTIAN, STRASBOURG.

THIS proximity to other countries is also apparent in the number of local dialects spoken by the inhabitants of this region. From the north through Picardy to the Ardennes, Picard and Walloon is spoken, as in Belgium, while the Alsatian spoken in Strasbourg resembles the Germanic dialect of Baden in German-speaking Switzerland. Language is the cement that binds people together and gives them a sense of belonging, because they share the secrets that only dialect can express.

Even more spectacular is the influence of foreign styles on the architecture of north-east France. The Carolingian empire was responsible for the octagonal design of the church at Ottmarsheim, similar to that of Charlemagne's chapel at Aachen. The Romanesque tradition, which lasted well after the flowering of the Gothic in the Île-de-France, is seen at its finest in the beautiful church at Marmoutier, and in the remarkable apse of the abbey at Murbach. Later, the influence of the Rhineland Renaissance is evident in the façade of Mulhouse's

(TOP RIGHT) House at Kaysersberg, a charming flower-decked town with a medieval atmosphere.

(RIGHT) Among its other treasures, Strasbourg's old city, along the river Ill and the canals, has wonderful timber-framed Alsatian houses. Some of most curious and best preserved examples are in the Petite France district, and in particular the Rue du Bain-aux-Plantes.

(OPPOSITE) Maison Kammerzell, Strasbourg. This jewel of carved wooden sculpture and frescoes was restored in 1954.

Hôtel de Ville, while the baroque tastes of Stanislas Leszczynski transformed Nancy, the historic capital of Lorraine, into an eighteenth-century gem with Jean Lamour's

inspired gilt ironwork. In Flanders, St-Quentin's richly decorated Hôtel de Ville is an astonishing example of the late Gothic, while on the belfries of Arras and Bergues the Flanders lion has replaced the traditional weathercock. In Lille, the Vieille Bourse is an outstanding Baroque palace, and the Gothic arcades and gables of the houses in the Grand'Place in Arras are reminiscent of Bruges.

(OPPOSITE) Grand'Place, Arras. The grandeur of this square is set off by the modest height of the buildings that surround it.

(TOP) The gilt-embellished ironwork of Jean Lamour in the Place Stanislas, Nancy.

(ABOVE) Foyer of the Opéra, Lille, built at the beginning of this century in the Louis XVI style.

Beauty of the cathedrals

THE greatest architectural achievements of northern France, however, are the Gothic cathedrals. Rivalling those of the Île-de-France in grandeur and beauty, their vertiginous soaring lines make them the boldest of all thirteenth-century constructions. The cathedral at Amiens, a palace of stone whose pillars soar to the roof-vaults, has the highest nave in France. The most famous cathedral is at Reims, for it traditionally served as the coronation church of the kings of France. At Metz, the warm golden Jaumont stone lights up the immense bays of the cathedral's transept; and the pink Vosges sandstone of Strasbourg's Notre-Dame was much admired by Goethe. The perfect elevations of these buildings uplift the soul, and their pure beauty is an inspiration to faith. All the delicate traceries of lacework can be seen, in stone, at St Wulfram's church in Abbeville, at Notre-Dame-de-l'Epine and in the abbey church at Avioth.

North-east France was also in the forefront of medieval monasticism, and various currents of religious thought had their origins here. The most famous of the religious orders was founded in the twelfth century by St Bernard at Clairvaux, in Champagne, the first Cistercian abbey. Other religious leaders of the time included the tragic lovers Héloïse, later abbess of the convent of the Paraclete, and her instructor Abelard, and Herrade de Landsberg, abbess of Niedermunster, the famous abbey founded by St Odile.

(ABOVE) Notre-Dame, Amiens. Begun in 1220 and completed 68 years later, this Gothic cathedral has the highest nave in France.

(RIGHT) The world-famous Smiling Angel, Reims Cathedral.

(OPPOSITE) The Gothic nave, Reims Cathedral.

Museum towns

THE towns and cities of northern France also contain a wealth of treasures. Today, the museum showcases house a range of art, from medieval times up until the present. No visit to Lille is complete without seeing the Flemish primitives in the Musée des Beaux Arts. In Colmar you can stand and wonder at Grünewald's sublime Isenheim altarpiece in the Musée Unterlinden. Both Troyes and Reims were famous for their school of sculptors; the smiling angel in the cathedral at Reims is one of the great emblematic achievements of Gothic art. At the turn of the century, Nancy gave its name to a whole school of craftsmen, led by Emile Gallé, who produced the delicately flowered Art Nouveau glassworks, ceramics and furniture admired in all the capitals of Europe during the Belle Époque.

The towns have also produced their share of famous writers, including Maurice Barrès, from Charmes in the Vosges, Chrétien de Troyes, from the town after which he is named, Denis Diderot from Langres, Verlaine from Metz, Marceline Desbordes-Valmore from Douai and many more. Today, the important university towns of Reims, Lille and Strasbourg keep alive intellectual and artistic traditions with a vigorous and flourishing cultural life.

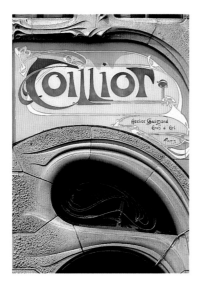

(ABOVE) Art Nouveau detail, Maison Coilliot, Lille, by Guimard.

(LEFT) Dining-room by Vallin, Musée de l'École de Nancy, Nancy. This splendid room, with its painted ceiling and leather wall decoration in a delicate floral design by Prouvé, illustrates the changes in middle-class interiors at the beginning of this century.

(RIGHT, ABOVE AND BELOW) Many of Nancy's commercial buildings and private houses were influenced by the Art Nouveau style. A glass roof with clematis at the Crédit Lyonnais bank, by Jacques Gruber, 1901; and a house on the Quai Claude-le-Lorrain, by Émile André, 1903.

(ABOVE) The Alsatian village of
Riquewihr prides itself on the fine
Riesling which has been produced by its
population for centuries. The vintners'
houses form a picturesque unity with
their mixture of red sandstone, brick,
timbering, painted façades and
balconies of flowers.

(RIGHT) Autumn colours in the
champagne vineyards.

The vineyards

CARVING ON A BARREL, THE WORK OF THE SCULPTOR GALLÉ, IN THE CAVE POMMERY, REIMS.

Vertical perspectives and straight lines are special features of this part of France. They are seen everywhere: in cathedral elevations, in towering belfries, in rows of crosses in military cemeteries, in the geometry of Vauban's fortresses, as well as in hillsides planted with vines, in rows of poplars and in the immense forests where shafts of sun pierce the foliage with translucent light.

Here, wine is king and the grape a symbol of wealth. The long and fertile strip of earth that stretches from the Belgian and German border, in the north, to the Île-de-France, Burgundy and the Jura in the south, contains the two great wine-producing areas of Champagne and Alsace. In centuries-old tradition, the vines are tended with the care and perseverance for which the inhabitants are renowned.

The vineyards also reflect the changing beauties of the seasons. In winter, long feathers of blue smoke from the little heaters placed at the foot of the vines of Champagne's Côte des Blancs rise into the sky through veils of mist. In spring, young vine leaves cloak the hillsides in green. In summer, insects hum around the swelling clusters above a dry soil that cracks underfoot. And finally, in autumn, the first flights of starlings announce the harvest. This is the most beautiful time of year, the season of Bacchus, the god of wine, when the black and yellow grapes glisten under the ruddy leaves. Although it is a time of hard labour, it is also one of joy.

Autumn is the month to take the road that winds through the vineyards from Marlenheim to Thann, past old and ruined castles outlined against the sky. This is also the best time to visit the chain of picturesque Alsatian wine villages like Eguisheim, with its half-timbered houses, oriel windows and red geraniums, or to stroll through the narrow, twisting streets of Obernai at the foot of Mont Ste-Odile. The Preiss-Zimmer house at Riquewihr, a small town famous for its Riesling and its picturesque houses with flower-decked balconies, and the extraordinary storks' nests at Hunawihr are other sights which should not be missed.

The vineyards of Champagne are some of the most serious and prestigious in the whole of France. Compared with the baroque noise and fervour of the vineyards of Alsace, they have a positively monastic reserve. It was, indeed, monks who famously perfected the blends and techniques to produce champagne, surely one of the wonders of the world. Dom Pérignon worked as cellar-master at Hautvillers, which today is decorated with hundreds of painted wrought-iron signs above its basket-handle gates.

The most famous cellars of all are at Épernay, the real capital of champagne, and at Reims. Visitors have only to walk through the miles of galleries hollowed out of the chalk, breathe in the heady scent of the wine and see the perfectly aligned rows of bottles carrying the great names of Moët et Chandon, Veuve Cliquot and Taittinger in order to absorb the peace and serenity of an atmosphere unaltered for four hundred years. To appreciate the true worth of champagne, you have to watch the *remueurs* who come to give the bottles an eighth of a turn every day for six months. Observing this underground hive of activity gives some inkling of what goes into the making of this world-famous sparkling wine. Champagne is rightly called the wine of gods and kings. Drunk from slender glasses that hold all its crisp bouquet, fine flavour and sparkle, it is the classic drink for every celebration, whether drunk as a toast to a freshly baptized baby or to the health of a newly married couple.

(BELOW) Bottles of champagne at Rilly-le-Montagne, south of Reims.

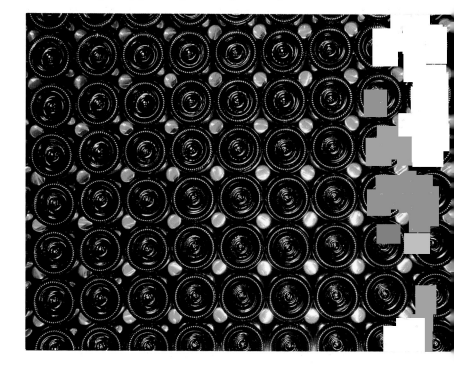

The forests

WOOD STACKED FOR WINTER
IN THE ARDENNES.

As so often is the case in unusual landscapes, the forests of north-east France are peopled with phantoms and strange beings. Legends abound and amongst the ruins of an ancient castle or at the edge of a wood it should come as no surprise to meet witches or forest imps. At Hohneck, it is even claimed by some that there is a giant who lies buried.

On the Montagne de Reims, dwarf beeches known as the 'Scythes of Verzy' show a disconcertingly twisted deformity. In the forest of St-Gobain, priories and abbeys were founded in order to convert a pagan nature to Christianity. The Argonne forest has lost nothing of its fantastical combinations of hills, plateaux and gorges, though it has seen many a battle – as the scars of the Haute Chevauchée trenches of the First World War still show. Compiègne's famous royal hunting forest was where Marie Antoinette of Austria was first introduced to the future Louis XVI. Its tall beeches, green vales, peaceful lakes, magnificent avenues and villages tucked into clearings were much favoured by Napoleon III and the Empress Eugénie as well as by their court.

The dense forest of the Vosges is more majestic, with its varied mixture of fir, larch, beech and pine. From the summit of the Grand Ballon, the highest point of the Vosges mountain range at 1,424 metres, a vast panorama opens out across the southern Vosges, the Black Forest and, on a clear day, the Jura and the Alps. Towards the summits the forests give way to rich pastures, the Hautes Chaumes. Even in misty weather, the forest of the Vosges still looks beautiful in a harmony of colours, its scent sealed in the little resin-flavoured sweets called *sucs des Vosges*. In the late summer, bilberry bushes cover the forest floor under the towering pine trees, turning the forest blue.

With the arrival of the first snows of winter, the skiers gather on the slopes of the Donon massif where the silence is unbroken, save for the sound of snow falling from the branches and the piercing cries of birds of prey.

The final triumph of winter comes with the illumination of a great Christmas tree around which expectant children await the arrival of St Nicholas, the Father Christmas of the north-east.

(BELOW LEFT) The knotted trunk of a contorted beech, whose branches form curious umbrella shapes, at Faux de Verzy, Montagne de Reims.

(BELOW) Château du Haut-Andlau; built in the fourteenth century and restored two hundred years later.

(OPPOSITE) The beauty of autumn in the Vosges countryside.

Festivals and Festivities

THE people of north-east France enjoy a strong sense of solidarity and hospitality. No journey is complete without a good meal and, in the difficult conditions of a long hard winter, friends will gather for an occasion or throw a party at the slightest excuse. Both festivals and folklore are full of the joys of living.

In Alsace and Lorraine, February is carnival time, when children put on disguises and go knocking on the doors for sweets and tidbits. The same tradition exists in Champagne and in the north, at Equilhen and Cassel, where giant figures are paraded through the streets. These enormous mascots have their origins in the history of a particular city or region: at Douai, for instance, the biggest and oldest of the giants, Gayant, bestrides the streets in fifteenth-century costume with his wife Marie Gagenon, while Lille parades its legendary founders Lydéric and Phinaert.

Pilgrimages are frequent in these lands, where faith and hard work go hand in hand. Boulogne celebrates Notre-Dame-du-Grand-Retour, who brings back lost ships, peace and soldiers taken prisoner: the name 'great return' refers to well-earned happiness. Mont-Ste-Odile is undoubtedly the most visited site in the whole of Alsace. Every year it attracts thousands of pilgrims who flock to the place where the saint escaped her father's cruelty by slipping into a miraculous opening in the rock.

The sanctuary of Notre-Dame-de-Sion on the Colline Inspirée, symbol of Lorraine's resistance to Prussian annexation in 1870 and one of the region's best-known viewpoints, also attracts considerable crowds.

Throughout the region the innumerable *ducasses* and *kermesses*, originally religious celebrations of a town's or

(ABOVE) Gayant and his wife Marie Gagenon, the giants of Douai. Gayant is the oldest and most popular of all the giants in the north-east.

(RIGHT) Dart feathers. These arrows, 50 or 60 centimetres long, are aimed at a target made up of a bundle of dense straw.

(OPPOSITE) In the north, it is difficult to keep count of the number of fairs, ducasses and kermesses, all occasions for having a good time.

village's local patron saint, have become opportunities for fairs and guild processions. At Béthune, the *Charitables*, the blacksmiths' guild, wearing two-pointed hats and black frock coats with sky-blue lapels, carry coffins from the church to the cemetery. At Ribeauvillé, the wandering musicians of Minstrels gather to honour their master, the lord of Ribeaupierre, on *Pfifferdaj*, the first Sunday of September.

Nowadays, great festivities also accompany traditional sports such as archery and perch shooting (*papegai*), where the target is suspended from the top of a pole. Darts are played in many cafés, there are famous cock-fights and pigeon-racing is popular. There is always a warm and cheerful atmosphere, with songs sung in Picard and Alsatian dialects, red and black traditional Alsatian costumes and stands selling pretzels, pancakes and waffles.

Beer and wine are celebrated in festivals at Arras in honour of Gambrinus, the king of beer, and at Schiltigheim, near Strasbourg. In early July, the harvest festival under the protection of St Urban takes place at Wangen in Alsace, and in Champagne there are festivals of St Vincent in the vineyards.

May is celebrated almost everywhere in this region: this might be in the form of a beribboned branch hung on the beloved's door, or a young tree planted to mark a birth, a wedding, a victory or a harvest.

In the tradition of the great medieval fairs of Champagne or the Grande Braderie in Lille – a gigantic flea-market which still takes place today – people have always gathered to do business and to make merry. All night long, miles of pavement are given over to traders and stallholders who tease the passers-by, while the restaurants and cafés of Lille's Place Rihour ply them with

mussels and white wine, vying with each other to build the largest pile of mussel shells outside their door.

Celebrations mean eating well and drinking well. At all times of day, people gather in the *estaminets*, the cafés of the north, for a beer, a coffee with chicory, or a *bistouille*, coffee with a dash of alcohol. Keen judges of good food, they sit in the brasseries that line the main squares of northern towns or the great hostelries of Alsace, where the vine shoots crackling in the fireplace banish the cold and damp. They are waiting for great dishes of *choucroute* to appear – to be washed down with beer or Riesling – or the thick and nourishing stews of Lorraine and Champagne.

At family gatherings people do justice to the local cuisine: *quiche lorraine*, *flamiche* and *flammekueche*; chicken and wild mushrooms; eel stews; tripe from Cambrai; *craquelots*, smoked herrings from Dunkerque; or *andouillettes*, tripe sausages from Troyes. No menu is too long for these *gourmands*. The main course is followed by the ripe cheeses of Munster or Maroilles, and then, to round off the meal, there might be a great plum tart with a glass of champagne, raspberry liqueur or gin. On winter evenings, when the days are short and the frost forms on the windows, what better consolation than to dip slices of *cramique* or *kougelhopf*, great slabs of bread and butter, into a steaming bowl of hot chocolate or to bite into delicious buttered pastries?

The festive spirit is typical of north-east France, where people enjoying themselves around a table groaning with food give the impression of having just stepped out of a Breughel painting of just such a feast.

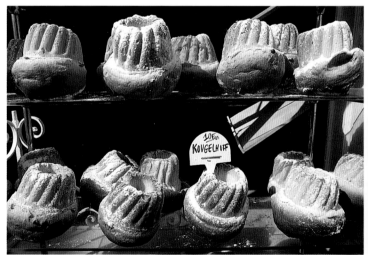

(TOP LEFT) *On the stove of a café in Flanders are the two traditional drinks of the region: beer and coffee.*

(LEFT) *Regional produce of the Ardennes.*

(ABOVE) *The famous Kougelhopf cake of Alsace.*

(OPPOSITE) *Old-fashioned bakery, Boulogne.*

Burgundy and Franche-Comté

Romanesque churches, tiled red roofs, a colourful countryside and wonderful vineyards make this a province to discover.

POLYGONAL ROMANESQUE
BELLTOWER, ANZY-LE-DUC.

THE third Sunday in November is a red-letter day for the whole of Burgundy, for it is the day on which the wines of the Hospices de Beaune, produced from 58 hectares of Burgundy's finest vineyards, are sold at public auction in Beaune.

Although the proceeds from this charitable event go towards the upkeep and modernization of the medieval Hôtel-Dieu hospital, the prices in the sale provide an indicator of the trend for all the other wines of the region. This conjunction of wine, art and history in a single place on a single day in autumn is a remarkable symbol of the pride and glory of Burgundy.

(ABOVE) Interior of Notre-Dame, Semur-en-Auxois. Many times rebuilt, this church was restored in the nineteenth century by Viollet-le-Duc.

(RIGHT) Beaune is not only the centre of Burgundy's prestigious wine industry but is also a beautiful historic town full of art treasures.

The monastic tradition

IN the Middle Ages Burgundy was at the forefront of a remarkable revival of monasticism centred on Cluny and Fontenay.

The seeds for the future fame and prosperity of the abbey of Cluny were already present at its foundation in 910. Deep in the vast forests of the Grosne valley, the abbey was situated in a frontier zone between lands ruled by the Carolingian king of France, Charles III, and the territories of Ludwig IV of Germany. The abbey's independence was absolute: it was subject to no authority other than that of the Pope. At a time when the great feudal estates were being broken up, it answered to no one but its elected abbot. In an unstable and unscrupulous world groping for a new sense of direction, it represented in exemplary fashion the ideals of asceticism and culture contained in the rule of St Benedict.

Cluny's development was rapid, its prestige immense and its influence pre-eminent at a crucial moment in the history of Western culture. In less than a hundred years, the abbey had amassed considerable political power as well as property. For two and a half centuries the leaders of this centre of monasticism were men of exceptional calibre and longevity, some of whom ruled for as long as sixty years. By the fourteenth century, however, the monks were failing to comply with the Benedictine rule and its ideal of poverty, and the Cluniac order declined.

The great abbey church at Cluny, which in its time was the largest Romanesque building in the Western world, was begun by St Hugh in 1088 and completed under Peter the Venerable in 1130. Its destruction began at the height of the French Revolution in 1798 and continued until 1823. All that remains today are the lower parts of two transept towers and two of the five bell-towers.

The abbey at Cîteaux was founded by Robert, abbot of Molesme, a few years before St Bernard of Clairvaux, who was born at Fontaine-lès-Dijon, joined it in 1112. Under Bernard's leadership the Cistercian order at Cîteaux aimed to restore the asceticism, spirituality and self-renunciation of the original Benedictine rule.

St Bernard, a contemporary of Peter the Venerable, the abbot of Cluny, was one of the great spiritual leaders of the Middle Ages – a writer, preacher, theologian, philosopher and statesman. Though physically diminished by fasting and self-mortification, he was quite tireless in dedicating an extraordinary will to the service of the Church.

After three years in Clairvaux, Bernard founded Fontenay, his 'second daughter', in 1118. The Abbaye de Fontenay, tucked away in an isolated valley in northern Burgundy, is the most evocative example of a self-sufficient

(RIGHT) Salle Capitulaire, Abbaye de Fontenay. An example of quadripartite vaulting, with decorated capitals, it leads to the eastern gallery of the cloister by way of a magnificent arcade.

(OPPOSITE) The elegant choir of the Sacré-Coeur basilica, a magnificent example of the Cluny school of architecture, at Paray-le-Monial.

Cistercian monastery of the twelfth century.

Fontenay is the architectural expression of St Bernard's ideas, forming the perfect setting for monastic life according to the rule of St Benedict. The equal division, in the twenty-four-hour day, between prayer, work and sleep found its physical equivalent in the functional arrangement of the buildings: church, cloisters, chapter house, scriptorium (where manuscripts were copied), dormitory and forge.

Fontenay's abbey church was begun in 1139 and completed eight years later. With its uncomplicated layout, square chancel and chapels, it is the first example of the 'monastic simplicity' in architecture that was called for by St Bernard.

Thanks to favourable conditions – numerous towns, rich abbeys and an abundance of building materials – the Romanesque school in Burgundy developed with an extraordinary vitality in the eleventh and twelfth centuries, not only in architecture but also in painting and sculpture. Enormous numbers of architects and artisans were employed on the building and decoration of the abbey at Cluny, and this was to have repercussions in religious foundations throughout the region and beyond.

The most striking example of the Romanesque is the abbey of St Philibert in Tournus. The architecture is powerful, sober and austere. The west front has the appearance of a castle keep: its loophole slits form dark shadows against the warm colour of the stone, and the bareness of the massive walls is relieved by slightly projecting Lombard bands. Inside, the luminous pink-coloured nave, with its splendid, tall, cylindrical pillars, is now lacking any decoration.

The church of Paray-le-Monial, built under the direction of St Hugh, is a replica of the great abbey church at Cluny. The influence of Cluny can also be seen at Charité-sur-Loire, at the cathedral of St-Lazare in Autun, at St Andoche in Saulieu and at Semur-en-Brionnais, the home town of St Hugh.

In opposition to the Cluny school, Burgundy has a whole series of churches of quite different character. The best

example is the basilica of Ste-Madeleine at Vézelay, one of the great pilgrimage churches of the Middle Ages. Its style represents a synthesis of true Burgundian Romanesque architecture. Built in the early twelfth century on a hill overlooking the river Cure, the Vézelay basilica differs from earlier buildings in the use of ribbed vaults in the nave, previously seen only in aisles. The great arches are surmounted directly by high windows which light up the nave. The semi-circular transverse arches supporting the vault are a notable feature, as is the use of alternating light and dark limestone in the arches.

The Cluny school of sculpture was the most significant development of the Romanesque period. On the capitals of the choir, the fluidity of the vegetal forms and litheness of the keenly observed human figures show a new interest in nature and man. The figures are draped in flowing tunics whose folds are a model of harmony and serenity.

Apart from its beautiful carved capitals, the church of Ste-Madeleine at Vézelay has in its narthex the sculpted tympanum depicting Christ sending the Apostles out into the world before his ascension into heaven. This masterpiece of the Burgundian Romanesque, dating from around 1120, has several features in common with the portal of the Last Judgement in the cathedral of Autun. The slightly earlier capitals of the nave and choir, with their vivid depictions of Biblical scenes and episodes from the lives of the saints, provided inspiration for the energetic and talented artists of St-Andoche in Saulieu.

At Berzé-la-Ville, the small Romanesque priory chapel has some celebrated frescoes in the apse. At the end of his life, St Hugh of Cluny lived nearby, and the Cluny influence is clearly evident in the Byzantine inspiration of the murals, which are painted on a blue ground. The Cluniac artists who worked at Berzé were directed by Benedictine painters from Monte Casino where the influence of the eastern Roman Empire survived until the eleventh century.

(LEFT) Basilica of Ste-Madeleine, Vézelay.

(RIGHT) Grape-harvesting scene, Les Riches Heures de la Duchesse de Bourgogne, fifteenth century, Chantilly, Musée Condé.

(TOP RIGHT) Carved capital known as the 'Mystical Mill', Vézelay.

(BOTTOM RIGHT) The Virgin of Autun, fifteenth-century Burgundian statue (Musée Rolin).

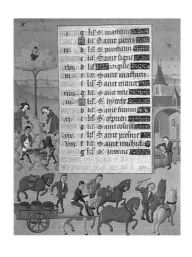

The dukes of Burgundy

THE exceptional scope of this monastic movement created a spiritual unity on which the great dukes of Burgundy during the fourteenth and fifteenth centuries were to build one of the most powerful states in Europe. The duchy of Burgundy was built up through a series of astute marriages. After the Treaty of Verdun, the Franche-Comté, or 'free county', then under the authority of the emperor of Germany, was attached by personal links to Burgundy, which had remained within the French sphere of influence.

Though the Capetian dukes continued to be very close to the kingdom of France, their primary concern until 1361 was to consolidate their duchy. The marriage in 1369 in Ghent of Philip the Bold, the first duke of Burgundy from the house of Valois, to Marguerite de Male, heiress of Flanders, Artois, Nevers and Franche-Comté, put the final touches to a policy which was to turn a patchwork of distinct fiefdoms into a vast, wealthy and structured entity of incomparable artistic achievement and influence. Above all, the marriage brought together two different cultures: Burgundy, with the great medieval heritage of Cluny, Tournus and Vézelay, and the Flanders of Ghent and Bruges.

Dijon became the southern capital of the new state, a counterweight to Ghent in the north. Here the duke attracted a brilliant court, including a large number of Flemish artists. Anxious to provide a burial place for himself and his successors, Philip the Bold founded the Chartreuse de Champmol in 1383, a magnificent building decorated by the finest artists of the time. His tomb (now in the Musée des Beaux-Arts) is a marvel of the Flamboyant style, its sides representing a cloister in which a train of hooded mourners wrapped in long cloaks forms the funeral cortège.

(ABOVE) Detail of the Well of Moses, Chartreuse de Champmol, Dijon. In this work by Claus de Werve, the angels under the cornice express their sorrow at the Passion.

(RIGHT) Hôtel Chambellan, Dijon. The central column of the Gothic staircase ends in a Flamboyant arch.

(OPPOSITE) Hôtel de Vogüé, Dijon. One of the principal parliamentary hôtels of Dijon, it was built by Étienne Bouhier at the beginning of the seventeenth century in an Italian Renaissance and Burgundian style. Its beautiful roofing of glazed tiles is clearly visible from a distance.

(*ABOVE*) *Great Hall, Hôtel-Dieu, Beaune. This immensely long room, which housed the sick and poor, has a magnificent arched ceiling in the shape of an upside-down ship's hull. The hangings, testers and bedding in a harmony of red and white tones make a striking arrangement.*

(*RIGHT*) *Hospice and Cour d'Honneur, Hôtel-Dieu.*

John the Fearless, spurred by political ambition into rebellion against the French king, was succeeded by Philip the Good, a great statesman who ruled for nearly fifty years. Philip allied himself with the English and in 1430 handed over to them for the enormous sum of 10,000 *livres* Joan of Arc, whom he had captured in Compiègne. A few years later, however, he came to an understanding with Charles VII at the Treaty of Arras and further enlarged his domains. Dijon thus became the capital of a powerful state and Burgundy entered a golden age.

Among the many painters attracted to Philip's court in Dijon were Claus de Werve, Henri Bellechose, Robert Campin and Roger van der Weyden, who gave their service just as Van Eyck was working for the duke in Bruges at the height of its Renaissance splendour. Never before had the Burgundian state been so powerful nor its court so lavish. On his wedding day in 1429, Philip the Good founded the Order of the Golden Fleece on the model of the English Order of the Garter.

The Hôtel-Dieu in Beaune was founded in 1443 by Nicolas Rolin, for forty years the duke's unfailingly zealous Chancellor, and his third wife Guigone de Salins. This hospital for the poor is a marvel of Burgundian-Flemish art and contains the polyptych of the Last Judgement, one of Roger van der Weyden's greatest altarpieces.

By the time Charles the Bold succeeded Philip in 1467 the balance of power in France had shifted and in Louis XI he found himself facing a stubborn, wily and remarkably effective monarch. By annexing Lorraine, Charles would have linked his southern and northern states, but his death at the siege of Nancy in 1477 marked the end of the Burgundian dynasty. His daughter Mary of Burgundy married the Hapsburg Maximilian, Holy Roman Emperor. The recovery of Burgundy and the other lands making up her dowry cost France more than two and a half centuries of diplomatic and military effort.

(RIGHT) The tombs of Philip the Bold and John the Fearless, who lies beside Margaret of Bavaria, rest on a slab of black marble supported by alabaster arches forming a 'cloister' under which is a crowd of mourners carved with realism and vitality.

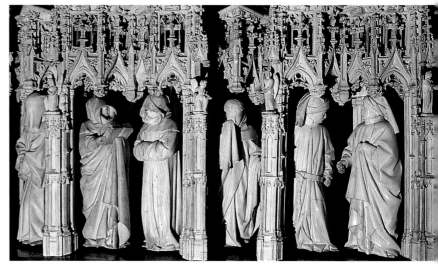

Franche-Comté: the Jura

PORTE NOIRE AND
CATHEDRAL, BESANÇON.

I N 1493, Emperor Maximilian of Austria granted Franche-Comté to his son Philip the Fair, who married Joan the Mad, heiress of Spain. Their son Charles V inherited Spain from his mother and Hapsburg lands, among them Flanders and Franche-Comté, from his father. In the sixteenth century Franche-Comté, having been successively part of the Holy Roman Empire and the Duchy of Burgundy, thus became a Spanish possession.

This era marked a high point in the province's commercial life, illustrated by the rise of the Granvelle family. Perrenot, a humble peasant from the Loue Valley, became Chancellor to Charles V; the palace he built for himself at Besançon between 1525 and 1545 is a fine example of domestic architecture.

When Louis XIV conquered Franche-Comté in 1674, he made Besançon the capital of the new French province. Aware of the vulnerability of his frontier, he ordered his engineer Vauban to make the city impregnable. The strategic importance of Vauban's citadel is best appreciated from the sentry-walk along the ramparts that encircle the promenades, the watch-towers and the two prominent look-outs named after the king and his queen.

The old Franche-Comté, a mysterious and hotly disputed land, today roughly corresponds to the uplands of the Jura (the word means forest). This mountainous region, with its folklore of werewolves, witches and fairies, is very different from neighbouring Burgundy. Its evergreen forests (La Joux, Levier, La Fresse, Le Massacre) and vast meadows form a pleasing landscape whose appeal is heightened by the sparkle of running water. There are foaming torrents, series of rapids and falls (Billaude, Flumen, Hérisson, Doubs), a multitude of little streams and the powerful resurgence of underground rivers at the source of the Loue and the Lison, as well as the dense network of the Rhône, the Doubs, the Ain and their tributaries (Valserine, Loue, Bienne, Albarine).

The calm surfaces of some seventy lakes (Bonlieu, Chalain, Nantua, St-Point) provide a contrast with all this movement, as do the reservoirs formed by the dams (Vouglans) that seem to transform the Ain valley into a giant staircase. Magnificent viewpoints (Grand Colombier, Colomby de Gex, Mont-Rond) offer panoramic vistas of typical Jura landscapes, with parallel valleys separated by ridges and linked by transverse valleys. The term Jurassic has passed into geological usage to describe these characteristic features, including the extraordinary natural amphitheatres, like the Cirques de Baume and de Consolation and the Roche du Prêtre, that are a simple lesson in geography.

(OPPOSITE) Waterfall, Baume-les-Messieurs. Water in the Jura takes many forms, from romantic, gushing torrents to peaceful lakes.

(RIGHT) Cirque de Ladoye. Nicknamed the 'ends of the world', these culs-de-sac are a feature of the Jurassic relief.

The world's finest wines

DRYING OF GRAPES FOR THE
VIN DE PAILLE, JURA.

SOUTH of Dijon stretches one of the world's most beautiful and best-known wine-growing regions, with Beaune almost at its centre, equidistant from Gevrey-Chambertin and Givry. The vineyards, first planted in Gallo-Roman times, were extended during the Middle Ages as forest and woodland were cleared away for monastic foundations.

The reputation of Burgundy wines grew in the fifteenth century along with the rise of the ducal court, but it was in the following century that the fortune of the great vineyards was decided as the monks mortgaged their lands and control passed into the hands of financial interests from the towns.

The 'Côte' is formed by a long, straight escarpment, deeply fissured in places, rising above the alluvial plain of the Saône. At its foot, depending on complex conditions of soil, drainage, exposure and microclimate, grow the vines whose grapes make the great wines; the most precious of the vineyards are enclosed by walls.

To the north is the Côte de Nuits, celebrated for its noble red wines (Nuits, Vosne, Vougeot, Chambolle, Morey, Gevrey, etc) made from the choice Pinot Noir grape, and to the south the Côte de Beaune, where the same grape makes other great red wines (Beaune, Pommard, Volnay, Chassagne-Montrachet,

(ABOVE AND RIGHT) The vine thrives best in a dry, warm and stony soil, where the water can filter through easily. Chalky ground produces wines, such as Côte de Nuits and Côte de Beaune, which have a good bouquet, are strong in alcohol and can be kept for a long time.

Santenay, Mercurey). The Chardonnay grape makes the finest of white wines (Meursault, Puligny-Montrachet, etc).

Here, as farther south in the region – around Mâcon – famous for its Pouilly-Fuissé, the vine rewards all the toil. In difficult conditions, the growers lavish their attentions on each plot, each plant, familiar with every inch of ground. These *vignerons* are famous for their individualism and attachment to their vines; it is only at the cost of unflagging thoroughness and care that the *grands crus*, heirs of a thousand years of know-how, reach the summits of perfection.

Great wines call for great food – a tradition maintained and enhanced by a long line of Burgundian chefs who have drawn their inspiration from authentic local produce. The tables of the great restaurateurs at Joigny, St-Père-sous-Vézelay, Saulieu, Dijon and Tournus, for instance, as well as those in other lesser known places, are graced by pâtés encased in pastry, pike *quenelles*, the delicate *poulet de Bresse*, snails and *coq au vin* – all providing an inexhaustible source of delight for any visitor with an interest in food and wine.

(ABOVE AND TOP RIGHT) Cherry trees in autumn, Irancy, south of Auxerre; the harvest of chestnuts in the Yonne.

(RIGHT AND FAR RIGHT) Café Auclair à Chapaize; fresco depicting scenes of the grape harvest at Buxy.

(OPPOSITE) Traditional spice shop selling spirits and confectionery in Dijon.

(ABOVE) *Traditional forest farm,
St-Trivier-de-Courtes, with maize
hanging out to dry in the open porch.*

(RIGHT) *An ancient dovecote.*

(FAR RIGHT) *A fortified farm in the
Yonne.*

(OPPOSITE) *Château de Sercy in the
valley of the Grosne.*

Burgundy past and present

THE unity of Burgundy suggested by the great medieval abbeys, the magnificent buildings erected by the great dukes and the vineyards is more the result of history than of geography. It should not, however, be allowed to mask the individual character of the very different smaller areas knitted together to form the province.

At Solutré, symbol of the area south of Mâcon, there is a celebrated prehistoric site. The settlement at Châtillon-sur-Seine is home to a huge sixth-century BC bronze vase, the 'Vix Crater'. Like the hill-camp of Bibracte on Mont Beuvray, it is an eloquent testament to the presence of the Gauls in France's eastern heartland.

To the north, Auxerre, capital of lower Burgundy on the banks of the Yonne, boasts the ancient abbey of St-Germain, whose crypt houses the oldest known frescoes in France. In Sens, the old houses still huddle around the vast bulk of St-Étienne, one of France's first Gothic cathedrals.

Between Auxerre and Autun, in the heart of Burgundy, lies the Morvan, a granite massif of poor soils, lonely farmsteads, scattered hamlets and extensive dark forests. Sheltering in a particularly wild and remote spot, like so many abbeys of the past, is the abbey of Pierre-Qui-Vire, which was built at the end of the last century.

Far removed from this windswept massif is the lush countryside of the Bresse plain, famous for its beef, pork and delicately flavoured poultry. The appearance of the isolated farms has not changed for generations and many of them still have an open porch for drying maize.

Visitors to the market town of Bourg-en-Bresse can admire the extraordinary church of Brou on its outskirts. In the early years of the sixteenth century Margaret of Austria, widow of Philibert the Fair, decided to transform the priory of Brou into a monastery, partly in fulfilment of a vow, partly to assert her status and partly to symbolize her love for her husband. The church, in exuberant late-Gothic style, contains a stone rood-screen, seventy-four choir-stalls and three splendid tombs.

(OPPOSITE) Notre-Dame-du-Haut, Ronchamp. Built by Le Corbusier in reinforced concrete, this chapel is famous for the purity of its curving lines. Here the architect broke with the rationalist movement and the rigidity of its formats; its design owes more to sculpture than to architecture.

(ABOVE) Sacré-Coeur church, Audincourt. The baptistry is inundated with purple and yellow light from Bazaine's stained glass windows.

(BELOW) Picking up on the thread of history, Taizé has today become an important ecumenical centre, a meeting place where one can pray, meditate and reflect in silence or in joyous communal celebrations.

Throughout the region there are magnificent castles housing priceless treasures. Those at Tanlay, Ancy-le-Franc, Sully, St-Fargeau and Cormatin are some of the finest examples, bearing witness to Burgundy's wealth and exceptional history.

If a link were to be made between earlier centuries and the present day, however, it is doubtless at Taizé that the connection should be sought. In the shadow of Cluny, heir to the great monastic tradition of Burgundy, this peaceful little village is today home to an ecumenical community whose fame has spread throughout the world. Bringing together thousands of young people from across Europe, Taizé is a place of prayer and dialogue, a source of hope and a symbol of brotherhood.

Rhône-Alps

The majestic Alps and powerful Rhône together form the link between the north and the south of Europe.

Mountains and water

A MOUNTAIN CHAPEL

THE Rhône runs west from Lake Geneva to the city of Lyon before heading purposefully south to the Mediterranean coast. Together with its tributary the Saône, this great river has long served as one of the major communications corridors of Europe. As it takes its course downstream, the landscape along its valley gradually changes. From the industrial area around Lyon the river runs through a succession of narrow gorges and broad basins planted with vineyards and orchards. To the north of Lyon lie the Beaujolais vineyards; to the west the Massif Central escarpment and the gorges cut by the Ardèche river; to the east the summits of Mont Blanc.

The Alps, overlooking the busy Rhône valley for their entire length, are undoubtedly one of the most majestic sights in France. Negotiating the steep hairpin bends, the traveller will be dazzled by the breathtaking vistas out over the plain; lakes sparkle in the distance and snow-covered Alpine peaks jut up into a cerulean sky. Likewise, the spectacular gorges cut by the Verdon and Ardèche rivers inspire awe. Although the steeply sloping roofs of the houses that cling to the mountainsides are a reminder of the harshness of the winters, the resorts of Chamonix, Megève and Courchevel draw devotees of winter sports from all over the world. In and out of season, from Évian to Grenoble, from Briançon to Mont Ventoux, from Lyon to Montélimar, each place has its own atmosphere and distinctive specialities.

The whole region, with its centuries of history, is like an unfolding drama which visitors can discover at their own pace. Whether skiing down the highest peaks of the Alps or dawdling along the romantic road that runs beside the Rhône, the landscape unfolds with the unfailing ability to thrill.

(TOP LEFT) The village of Balazuc, clinging to a cliff in a narrow pass in the Ardèche.

(CENTRE LEFT) Countryside round Burzet in the Ardèche, famous for its Good Friday procession.

(BOTTOM) The pass of Pierre Chatal, near Annecy.

(OPPOSITE) Canoeing in the Ardèche gorges. The Ardèche makes a succession of graceful meanders, at the bottom of a 30-kilometre-long deserted gorge between cliffs that occasionally rise to 300 metres.

The view from above

PUNCTUATED by the highest peaks in Europe, dotted with lakes and patterned with roads cut into the mountainside, the Alps stretch in a 1,000-kilometre arc from Nice to Vienna. The deep, wide valleys provide easy access. Villages, isolated farmhouses in alpine pastures and wayside chapels perch in an imposing landscape where the contrasts accentuate the splendour of the setting: only a few miles, for example, separate the peaceful shores of Lake Geneva from the soaring pinnacles of Mont Blanc, or the limestone cliffs of the Vercors from the Grésivaudan plain.

The Route des Grandes Alpes, running at an altitude of over 2,000 metres, is the most famous and most spectacular of the many roads through the French Alps. Linking Lake Geneva with the Riviera, it follows the skyline and rarely strays far from the frontier; it also offers a series of unparalleled views.

(OPPOSITE) View of the Col du Rousset, which marks the climatic boundary between the northern and southern Alps.

(LEFT) A fall of snow, near Aussois.

(ABOVE) The Mont-Blanc massif, the Aiguille du Midi and the valley of Chamonix below the Brévent.

STREET IN ANNECY.

The valleys of the northern Alps of Savoie, home to the marmot and chamois, are connected by high cols such as the Lautaret and Galibier passes. The valleys themselves, such as the Romanche and Maurienne, tend to be industrialized or serve as corridors for through traffic; market towns like Grand-Bornand in the Aravis valley or Boudin in the Beaufortain have grown up where the valleys broaden out into sunny terraced basins. The great lakes of Geneva, Annecy and Le Bourget lie at the foot of slopes covered with magnificent beech, pine and spruce forests.

At the crossroads of the Grésivaudan, where the Drac and Isère valleys meet, stands Grenoble, the economic, intellectual and tourist capital of the French Alps. The position of this city

is altogether exceptional: to the north lie the sheer cliffs of Néron and St-Eynard, outriders of the Chartreuse massif; to the west the towering escarpments of the Vercors dominated by the majestic peak of Le Moucherotte; to the east the dark chain of the Belledonne mountains, whose peaks are covered in snow for most of the year. Grenoble is a young and modern city; its museum of modern and contemporary art has few equals in Europe.

(LEFT) A typical church in the Maurienne valley.

(ABOVE) Lac du Bourget, Savoie, much loved by the Romantic poets.

(RIGHT) Lac d'Annecy framed by summits.

(OPPOSITE, TOP RIGHT) Cable-car, Fort de la Bastille, Grenoble.

(OPPOSITE, BOTTOM RIGHT) Musée de Grenoble, a model of sobriety, built on the banks of the Isère.

In Napoleon's footsteps

COLOURFUL FAÇADES AT
BARCELONNETTE.

THE southern Alps are drained by the great sub-Alpine furrow of the Durance. Arid and bare like Provence, their hillsides announce the arrival of more typically Mediterranean landscapes. Mont Ventoux dominates the Comtat plain, while the Verdon gorges score a huge gash across the last foothills of the Alps in upper Provence. Sheep farming, lavender growing and forestry are the principal activities of the inhabitants of high-altitude villages such as St Véran, which at about 2,000 metres is the highest settlement in Europe.

In the Embrunais, Queyras and Briançonnais, picturesque mountain chalets are dotted round the countryside. There are also some enchanting spots, like the turquoise lake behind the Serre-Ponçon dam. Other sights are the peak of La Bonnette, the charming little town of Barcelonnette in the heart of the Ubaye valley, and the astonishing rock formations of the Ecrins National Park.

If the northern Alps are subject to oceanic influences, the southern Alps belong to the Mediterranean. The dividing line between them runs through the Rousset, Croix Haute, Bayard, Lautaret and Galibier passes. The best, and certainly the most agreeable, way of crossing the southern Alps is to take the famous Route Napoléon, named after the path taken by the former emperor on his return to France from Elba. The route traces his journey from his departure at Golfe-Juan on the Riviera to his arrival at Grenoble.

Mont Ventoux, at nearly 2,000 metres, is the highest point of upper Provence. Splendid in its isolation, it is capped in winter with a sparkling mantle of snow. Its nickname, the 'windy one', comes from the mistral which blasts its summit with an unequalled force.

Further to the south, the Verdon, a tributary of the Durance with its source high up in the Allos Pass, has cut Europe's most spectacular gorge through the Castellane pre-Alps in a landscape that has resisted all human attempts to tame it. The Corniche Sublime, the tortuous scenic route on the south bank of the river, offers the most spectacular viewpoints, particularly down the vertiginous drops into the canyon below.

(OPPOSITE) The Route Napoléon at the high point of the village of Séranon.

(ABOVE) An immense field of lavender in the Valensole plateau.

(RIGHT) The Verdon gorges, upstream from the Lac de Ste-Croix. Even higher up is the Great Canyon, extending for 21 kilometres.

Majestic Mont Blanc

R ISING to a height of 4,807 metres, the Mont-Blanc massif
surpasses all other mountains in Europe. It earns its
reputation as a tourist attraction, however, for the wonderful
variety of sights offered by its domes, glaciers and needles. The
panorama from the central peak of the Aiguille du Midi is
staggering; it takes in the snowy splendours of Mont Blanc
itself, Mont Maudit, the Grandes Jorasses and the dome of the
Goûter, whose buttresses are buried deep in the ice. The Vallée
Blanche (also known as the Glacier du Géant) offers views of
the glacial amphitheatres whose flanks have been worn down
by the incessant attack of the ice. Another spectacular sight is
the Mer de Glace. This glacier, which has formed an
extraordinary sea of ice 14 kilometres long and 400 metres
thick in parts, ranks as one of the most surprising sights of the
entire Alps.

This strange, immense world of silence is also the
birthplace of mountaineering. After several unsuccessful
attempts, the first ascent of Mont Blanc was made in August
1786 by Dr Michael Paccard and Jacques Balmat, thus marking
the historical birth of this new high-risk sport.

Ski heaven

With blue sky and mountain backdrops, the Alps offer the skier
everything, from peaceful cross-country trails to exhilarating
downhill runs and the joys of powdery off-piste snow. The
skiing areas are quite remarkable, especially at Chamonix, from
which it is possible to take the cable-car up to the Aiguille du
Midi and ski down the Vallée Blanche glacier, even in summer.
Chamonix lies at the foot of the famous 'needles' of the same
name that tower 3,000 metres above it, at a place where the
glacial valley of the Arve widens out.

Courchevel, no less famous, is one of the largest and best
ski resorts in the world. Its north-facing slopes are guaranteed
snow from the beginning of December until May.

Other resorts are also highly valued for the quality of their
skiing and facilities, such as La Grave with its cable-car up to
the Meije glaciers, Avoriaz, now also famous for its film
festival, La Clusaz, Argentière, whose Grands Montets ski runs
are some of the most beautiful in Europe, and Les Contamines,
one of the most pleasant and restful resorts of the entire Mont
Blanc massif.

Every year, a thick mantle of immaculate snow descends
over the larch forests and valleys and the resorts come to life.
At Deux-Alpes, Méribel-Les-Allues, La Plagne and Tignes, ski

The awesome setting of Chamonix's high mountain.

lifts and cable-cars begin their incessant ballet, while, at Les Arcs, the Transarc takes experienced skiers to the foot of the Grive needle. At Megève, the most fashionable of all the resorts, celebrities from all over the world gather. Megève is the home of Émile Allais, downhill and slalom champion of the world in 1937.

The resorts of the southern Alps, though fewer in number, are renowned for their sunny weather and the gentleness of their climate. Serre-Chevalier, Vars-les-Claux and Les Orres are particularly suited to relaxing family holidays in pursuit of nature. Their cross-country snowshoe and ski trails are an inspiration to all who love the silence and freedom of wide-open spaces. As night falls, the lights of the villages twinkling on the heights make it seem as if the mountains are wearing strings of giant pearls.

If the Alps have become the number-one winter sports destination, it is without doubt not only because of their considerable natural advantages but also because of their strategic geographical position. Their closeness to national frontiers and their easy access from the great urban centres of Milan, Geneva and Lyon have contributed, to a large extent, to this development.

All forms of skiing and other mountain sports are possible in the Alps.

(TOP) Forests around Avoriaz.

*(ABOVE) La Clusaz, an important
resort of the Aravis massif.*

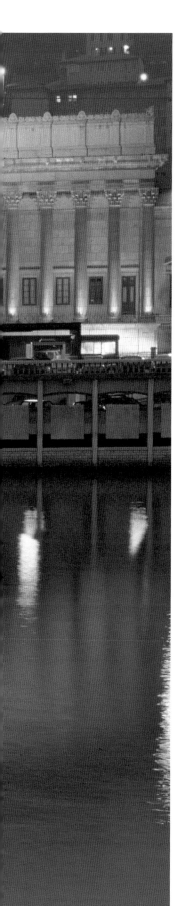

FAÇADES ON THE RHÔNE IN LYON

A unique position

Two thousand years of history and a unique position between the arteries of the Saône and Rhône have made Lyon France's second city. Its past periods of greatness, in Roman and Renaissance times, are a reminder that Lyon has always flourished, as at present, at times of great change, when it has been able to take maximum advantage of its exceptional situation. During the Middle Ages Lyon was one of the 'keys of the kingdom', bordering Savoie, Dauphiné, Italy and Germany on one side and Beaujolais, Burgundy, Languedoc, Forez and Auvergne on the other. When in 1419 the Dauphin and future king Charles VII, understanding the commercial value of such a situation, founded a twice-yearly fair there, Lyon became one of the world's great trading centres, attracting merchants from far and wide. From 1463, on the orders of Louis XI, the fair was held four times a year, encouraging the creation of the Exchange, the origin of the present Bourse, and the Conservatory Court, forerunner of modern commercial courts. Rabelais, then a doctor at the Hôtel-Dieu, arranged for the publication of *Pantagruel* and *Gargantua* to coincide with fairs in 1532 and 1534.

The ancient city of the Gauls has been the home of many inventions. In 1793 the Montgolfier brothers made one of the first balloon ascents. A century later, thanks to the genius of the Lumière brothers, cinematography was born and the first public projection took place in Paris in 1895. Finally, there were the sympathetic wooden puppets of the Lyon Guignol, whose fame spread throughout the whole of France. Their acerbic wit perfectly embodies the spirit of the people of Lyon.

(TOP RIGHT) A nineteenth-century building in the Place Ampère.

(CENTRE) The sixteenth-century Maison des Avocats, Old Lyon.

(OPPOSITE) The Palais de Justice beside the Saône.

(RIGHT) The glass roof of the Gare de Perrache.

A silk-weaving centre

A modern industrial city, Lyon is also a major international business centre. A staging-post on the road to Italy, at the cross-roads between central and eastern, northern and southern France, Lyon has been the capital of the silk industry since the sixteenth century. Previously, most silkstuffs had come from Italy. In 1804 Marie-Joseph Jacquard, perfecting a machine invented by Vaucanson, built a power loom which enabled a single worker to do the work of six workers, but it was the introduction of mechanical looms in 1875 that revolutionized the silk industry.

Life in Lyon is essentially simple, and little has changed as the years have gone by. The favourite distractions of its inhabitants are still walks along the banks of the Rhône and Saône and the ancient game of *boules*. The heart of the city beats in the peninsula and on the famous hills of Fourvière and Croix-Rousse. The old centre of Lyon around St Jean, St Paul and St Georges includes a number of remarkably well-preserved fifteenth- and sixteenth-century houses, connected by the narrow alleyways called *traboules*. Together they form an exceptional example of Renaissance urban architecture.

Over and above its regional influence, Lyon aims to be one of the most important European capitals. The elegant shops that line the Rue Gasparin and Rue du Président-Herriot, between the Place Bellecour and the Place des Terraux, rival those of Milan, Turin and Barcelona. Its cultural facilities, such as the Cité Internationale, its symphony orchestra and the new opera house, by the architect Jean Nouvel, are of world-class standard. But the time to grasp the true spirit of Lyon is over a pitcher of Beaujolais at the Brasserie Georges or Café des Négociants, in an atmosphere that is unfailingly friendly and relaxed.

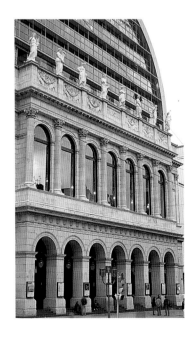

A lively and creative metropolis, Lyon has successfully blended contemporary styles with its rich architectural past.

(OPPOSITE, TOP) Notre-Dame de Fourvière viewed from the footbridge from the Palais de Justice.

(OPPOSITE, BOTTOM LEFT) Opéra de Lyon, remodelled by Jean Nouvel.

(OPPOSITE, LEFT) The corps de ballet in rehearsal.

(ABOVE) Inside view of the top of the Crédit Lyonnais tower, known locally as the 'crayon' (pencil). The 140-metre tower dominates the new district of Part-Dieu.

(RIGHT) Métro entrance in contemporary urban building materials.

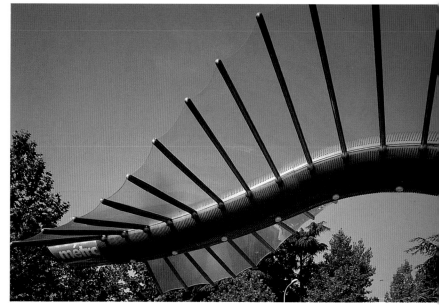

Food reigns supreme

THE fame of Lyon is due in no small measure to the quality of its restaurants, which have the reputation of being some of the finest in France. No visitor interested in French food should miss the opportunity of tasting Paul Bocuse's legendary Bresse chicken or truffle soup, or of dining at such famous restaurants as Orsi or Léon.

Lyonnais cooking, however, is above all simple and genuine. It is no accident that the greatest gourmets acknowledge Lyon to be the food capital of the world. The subtle flavours and textures of Lyonnais cooking would certainly not be what they are without the famous 'mothers', those robust cooks whose feminine touch is evident in the skilful association of products of the highest quality selected with uncompromising rigour. Pike *quenelles* grilled in the oven, *saucisson de Lyon* and the local poultry are all appetizingly full of flavour; and tripe dishes, liver pâtés, as well as other pork and ham products are best sampled in *bouchons*, bars typical of old Lyon and renowned for their warm atmosphere and temperamental landlords.

Lyon also has the good fortune of being in the heart of the Beaujolais and Côtes du Rhône wine-producing areas. The best-known wines are those of the Beaujolais and Mâconnais, with names like Brouilly, Juliénas, Morgon and Moulin à Vent. To the south of Lyon, the vineyards of the Côtes du Rhône stretch in a long ribbon on either side of the river. Condrieu and Château Grillet, elegant wines from the Côte Rôtie, are reckoned among France's finest white wines; St Joseph and Hermitage produce fine reds with a bouquet reminiscent of raspberries; further south, as the valley broadens out into Provence, are to be found the denser, heavier reds of Châteauneuf du Pape and Gigondas and the richly sweet muscat of Beaumes de Venise. Provence itself is best known for its fresh and light rosés.

(LEFT) *Brasserie des Brotteaux, Lyon, 1913. In its brasseries, bars and restaurants, famous chefs give free rein to their invention, earning Lyon the distinction of being one of the great gastronomic centres.*

(TOP RIGHT) *Enclosed in its ramparts, with narrow streets and ancient houses, Pérouges has preserved its medieval architecture.*

(RIGHT) *The annual market of lime flowers, on the first Wednesday in July, takes place at Buis-les-Baronnies.*

Rights of passage

THE RUINS OF THE CHÂTEAU DE CRUSSOL, ARDÈCHE.

LYON, so the saying goes, stands at the confluence of three rivers – the Rhône, the Saône and the Beaujolais. Even in ancient times, the Rhône below Lyon was a much-travelled waterway. From Marseille, the Greeks used the river to fetch tin from Cornwall. In Roman times, it became the main thoroughfare for the export of wine. For centuries the Rhône has been both a prime supply route and a means of transport for the towns and cities that have grown up along its banks.

The landscape of the Rhône corridor changes constantly over its 240-kilometre length. The Rhône is the largest and fastest-flowing river in France. South of Lyon, its course to the Mediterranean cuts a broad swathe of light between the slopes of the Massif Central and the pre-Alps. Fresh beauties are revealed at each meander, each curve, occasionally heightened by the strength and force of the mistral. Now overlooked by glowering cliffs, now forcing its way through narrow gorges, now basking in the expansive basins of its lower reaches as it heads towards Provence, the river offers a succession of spectacular scenery.

Between Lyon and Vienne, the famous industrial corridor soon gives way to the magnificent orchards that adorn the banks of the Rhône. A historical perspective is given by the Roman remains at Vienne and the ruins of castles perched on the heights, like the one at Crussol, a reminder of crueller and more violent times. Here towns tended to develop in pairs on opposing sides of the river. Churches and castles on top of vine-covered promontories add their idiosyncratic touch to the picture.

But without doubt the grandest view of the entire Rhône valley is the one from St-Romain-de-Lerps. From here, the horizon seems almost infinite, stretching over the Valence plain to the escarpments of the Vercors, scored with deep gullies, and beyond, in the far distance, to the great mass of Mont Blanc and the snow-capped summits of the Alps sparkling in the sun.

Rich in history, the region of the Alps and the Rhône valley, despite an environment sometimes hostile to humans, has never ceased to make the most of its natural resources and strategic geographical position. Today, the people of Lyon proudly display all the talents and advantages of belonging to a major economic, industrial, financial and cultural centre. The dynamism and enterprise of the former capital of the Gauls continue and Lyon still provides France with its leaders. A few miles away, top-class skiers meet on the slopes of some of the world's most famous ski resorts.

From the Haute Corniche of the Ardèche gorges to the cellars of the Beaujolais, from the steep slopes of Alpine valleys to the orchards of Provence, the glories of nature are displayed in all their grandeur along the Rhône corridor. Day after day, year after year, century after century, the majestic mountains of the Alps watch jealously over the sunlit banks and rapid currents of the Rhône so that mankind may admire this unique river for centuries to come.

(RIGHT) The Rhône at Tain-l'Hermitage. Powerful, fast and full, the Rhône is the most majestic of French rivers. South of Lyon, it heads towards the Midi, between the Massif Central and the pre-Alps.

(OPPOSITE) A rushing torrent near Entremont-le-Vieux, Savoie.

The Centre: Auvergne,
Berry, Limousin,
Périgord, Quercy

*Mountains, volcanoes, high plateaux, valleys and rich farmland make
for a varied countryside where it is still possible to find the unusual,
the authentic and the art of living.*

The green heart of France

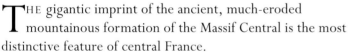

THE gigantic imprint of the ancient, much-eroded mountainous formation of the Massif Central is the most distinctive feature of central France.

Visible from the top of the Puy de Sancy, rising to nearly 2,000 metres at the heart of the volcanic landscape of the Auvergne, are the spectacular volcanoes of the Monts Dore, Monts Dômes and Cantal. These time-weathered ranges, formed by a sequence of eruptions and successive flows of lava, resemble great waves frozen in motion, their strong contours softened and blurred. They have none of the triumphant thrust of the younger Pyrenean or Alpine peaks, but their imposing bulk, a defining influence on the landscape and the people, is a reminder of a geological time-scale in which centuries pass in the blink of an eyelid.

Other uplands, forming a stepped concentric circle of moorland, pasture and forest around these summits, make for rough terrain and a harsh climate. They are the Artense, Margeride and Aubrac plateaux and the mountains of the Livradois, Forez and Bourbonnais, separated by the Limagnes, lower-lying, fertile plains drained by the rivers of the Dore and the Allier.

The alternation of bare granite uplands, out of which rise volcanic cones, and cultivated plains, where most of the towns and cities are concentrated, is the principal characteristic of the unusual and varied landscape of the Auvergne. The often blue-tinted light of these high central ranges give the horizons of the province a particular softness and charm.

(OPPOSITE) A road lined with centuries-old trees in Dordogne.

(ABOVE) The chain of volcanoes with the Puy de Dôme in the background. Along their 30-kilometre length, the Monts Dômes have a range of 112 extinct volcanoes, little changed in shape since the time when they were active.

(TOP RIGHT) The meandering Queuille in the Sioule valley. In the bend of the river the near bank is steep and rocky; on the other side, the river tightly hugs the wooded spine of the Murat peninsula.

(RIGHT) The river Ouysse in a deep valley to the north of Gramat, Lot.

(*ABOVE*) *Apremont-sur-Allier, a charming village at the foot of an impressive stronghold.*

(*FAR LEFT*) *A traditional game of skittles.*

(*LEFT*) *The imposing ruins of the Château de Commarque.*

(*OPPOSITE, TOP*) *Autumn colour along the river Queuille.*

(*OPPOSITE, BOTTOM*) *The Vézère valley at Les Eyzies-de-Tayac.*

From sources high up in the Massif Central flow countless
small rivers. As they make their way across the undulating
terrain of the outlying regions of the Auvergne, the
countryside changes. For the nineteenth-century writer
George Sand, who spent much of her life in Berry, they were
one of the beauties of the mountains: 'They are discreetly
hidden and small in size, to be sure, but vast in their
insinuations and perspectives, and infinitely happy in their
easy, fleeting motion...' (*Promenades autour d'un village*).

The great stretches of *bocage* in the Bourbonnais and the
Limousin are given over to grass, trees and water. The rivers
run through broad and narrow valleys of woods and pastures.
From the crystalline rocks of the Massif Central, they enter
the limestone plateaux of Berry and Périgord which herald
the Paris and Aquitaine basins. There is a great variety of
relief: the low and relatively flat land of Berry is devoted to
large-scale arable farming; in Périgord and Quercy the
causses, or upland plateaux, are deeply-riven. Clay
depressions, retaining the moisture, create a landscape of
ponds and lakes that are home to a thousand varieties of
wildlife.

All of these areas have been bitterly disputed through the
ages. The countryside, which is dotted with ruined castles
bearing the scars of feudal strife, inspires fierce loyalty.

The memories of the land go hand in hand with those of
its people – not only the barons who fought to possess it, but
also the peasants who lived on it and cultivated it. It is a place
where things take time, where what is best cannot be
hurried. The Auvergne, Limousin, Périgord and Berry are
regions with a deeply rooted rural tradition. This is most
clearly reflected in the robust local cuisine that relies on the
produce of the land, the tradition of craftsmanship and the
strength of ancestral beliefs, in which saints and sorcerers
coexist quite happily.

Long regarded as typical of France at its most traditional,
these regions are no longer as remote as they once were.
Motorways have been built and airports opened. Over the
years they have attracted numerous writers and artists who
have always acknowledged the strength of their attachment.
The Massif Central and its rim are famous for the plentiful
supply of springs and for the marketing and bottling of
mineral water. Thanks to the region's spas, tourist facilities
and healthy environment, it is a favourite destination for
holidaymakers seeking to recharge their batteries with the
pleasures of simple living and fresh air.

Autumn, with its softly luminous light, is perhaps the best
time of all to explore this land which has so many
unsuspected delights up its sleeve.

The volcanic massif

WHEN it comes to looking at volcanic formations, the visitor has a plethora of choices. The Auvergne represents a reservoir of such sites, particularly in the Monts Dôme, which are remarkable for the variety and strangeness of shapes and forms. Here can be seen craters, cones and steep-sided domes known as *puys*. Lava flows have solidified into needles on emerging from the earth, like the Puy Griou at the centre of the ancient Cantal volcano, or created vast upland tracts of fertile pasture and arable land known as *planèzes*. Some flows have filled whole valley floors, protecting the softer land from the erosion wearing away the hills around and giving rise to the phenomenon of relief inversion, as for example the plateau of Gergovie, the mountain of La Serre and the superb mound of Polignac.

There are marvellous panoramic views from several volcanic spurs or necks, illuminated at night: for example,

from Bonnevie, Bredons and Chastel at Murat, from Montgaçon and Montpensier overlooking the Limagne plains, and from the strange peaks of Le Puy-en-Velay topped by curious domed churches.

Lava flows are also responsible for the 'organ pipe' formations of the Roches Tuilière and Sanadoire in the Monts Dore and for the peak of Espaly in the Velay district.

(LEFT) Corrèze.

(ABOVE) The chapel of St-Michel d'Aiguilhe, Le Puy-en-Velay, at the summit of a giant needle of lava which spouted 80 metres up towards the sun.

(OPPOSITE, TOP) Massif du Sancy.

(OPPOSITE, BELOW) Lac Pavin. Its almost circular shape is due to a volcanic eruption.

The volcanic activity, obstructing valleys and breaking up the ground, has created a great number of lakes which reflect like mirrors in the landscape. Few of them, however, achieve the scintillating beauty of Lac Pavin, set like a jewel in the steep, wooded slopes of its crater. The legend that throwing a stone into the lake would cause terrible storms, whence its name (*pavens* in Latin means terrible), seems to be belied by its transparent waters which are full of freshwater trout and char.

In the upper valley of the Dordogne, whose fast and capricious currents were formerly plied by skilled boatmen, in the valleys of the Creuse and Truyère and the gorges of the Cère and Maronne, vast man-made lakes have been created. The damming of the waters has enhanced such places as Crozant and Bort, where the Château de Val rears its pepperpot turrets on a rocky island.

Roads built to serve hydro-electric power plants have made

these hitherto little-known sites more accessible. Most of the lakes and dams are in valleys whose beauty has attracted painters and writers. The Creuse valley between Fresselines and Gargilesse was depicted on canvas by Armand Guillaumin and Claude Monet, and in words by George Sand. From the fortified town of Domme, the writer Henry Miller described the valley of the Dordogne as being 'as close to heaven on earth as you could get'. The tortuous course of the lower Lot valley encircles ancient cities like Cahors and makes its way along cliffs and promontories to whose sides cling exquisite villages such as St-Cirq-Lapopie. The caves of the Vézère valley, designated a world heritage site, have witnessed thousands of years of human occupation.

The limestone plateaux of the Périgord and Quercy soak up rainwater like a sponge. The water, infiltrating the ground, forms underground galleries, rivers, lakes and domes which can collapse to form chasms as at Padirac, a veritable encyclopaedia of the fascinating effects of water. In some caves, the pillars, stalagmites and stalactites have created fantastic shapes which defy the laws of gravity and equilibrium. Here the visitor can enter a timeless, entrancing world whose magic is enhanced by concealed lighting. The Grotte du Grand Roc, high above the river at Les Eyzies-de-Tayac, has caves of such various colours and eccentric formations that they seem almost to be made of living matter.

Most of these caves were explored in the late nineteenth and early twentieth centuries, their discovery having been largely a matter of chance. The cliffs of the Vézère valley are full of these shelters and shrines of prehistoric man – an archaeologist's paradise.

An historic landscape

NEANDERTHAL MAN, LES EYZIES-DE-TAYAC

Fʀᴏᴍ the beginning, the Vézère and Creuse valleys have offered hospitable conditions for human survival: protection from the cold, proximity to rivers full of fish and the chance of trapping game in the narrow valleys.

Studies of the Périgord caves have helped to establish the first classification of the various ages of prehistory. Shelters hollowed out at the base of limestone cliffs served as prehistoric dwelling-places; the caves, whose entrances were generally halfway up the cliffs, probably served as shrines. Nobody visiting these caves can fail to be moved and impressed by the works of art of the Magdalenian period – the hand-stencils and dappled horses at Pech-Merle, the bison, reindeer and horses at Font-de-Gaume, and the powerful bulls and stags with outsize antlers at Lascaux II, the full-scale replica of the Lascaux caves once described as the 'Sistine Chapel of prehistory'. While scholars may continue to debate the interpretation of the paintings, engravings and sculptures, there can be no doubt that they represent a deliberate and conscious art.

Apart from the caves, there are other eye-catching sights. For on top of volcanic spurs overlooking rivers and dominating

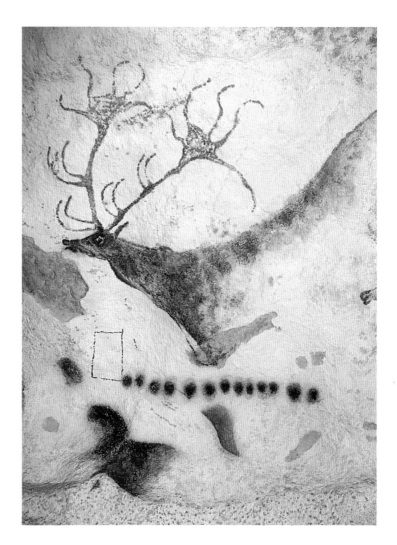

(OPPOSITE) The chasm of Proumeyssac. The flow of water continues to feed the extraordinary stalactites and stalagmites.

(TOP RIGHT AND RIGHT) The Lascaux cave is one of the most important prehistoric sites in Europe for the quantity and quality of its paintings.
Deep in the limestone of the Périgord Noir, the cave extends for 150 metres and is a bestiary of bulls and bisons.

the landscape are the ubiquitous ruins of fortresses and castles, sometimes glaring in defiance at one another across the frontier between two spheres of influence. The history of the region records scuffles between the barons of the Auvergne, the century-long confrontation between Capetian and Plantagenet forces, skirmishes between Catholics and Huguenots and the banditry of highwaymen and outlaws.

Everywhere are the traces of a turbulent past: the romantic ruins of Crozant, the towers of Merle, the fortress of Alleuze, the ruins of the Château de Polignac, home of the warrior 'kings of the mountains', the castles of Murol and Turenne, seat of a great line of noblemen, the strongholds of Tournoël, Anjony and Culan and the fortresses of Castelnaud, Beynac-et-Cazenac, Bonaguil and Castelnau-Bretenoux.

History has not been kind to these former bastions, dwelling-places in times of war, and few of them have remained intact: some were transformed by later owners according to the taste of the day, while others were quickly rendered obsolete by the progress in artillery power.

Later, when members of the bourgeoisie rose to fill the ranks around the king, there were further changes to the style of domestic living. Jacques Coeur, the wealthy local trader who became Charles VII's minister of finance, built himself a sumptuous Gothic palace in Bourges, with towers and turrets that were merely ornamental.

The influence of Loire Valley architecture can be seen in the châteaux Meillant, Villegongis and Valençay where stylistic change was allied to a growing taste for comfort and luxury. The Berry remained close to the centre of power; at the end of the Middle Ages an infinitely delicate flowering of the Gothic style represented a transition to the refinements of the Renaissance. Splendid residences and elegant chapels graced the capital cities of Charles VII, mocked as the 'king of Bourges', and Jean, Duc de Berry, who made Bourges a centre of the arts to rival Dijon, thus closing the great chapter of Gothic art and architecture.

The extraordinary cathedral of St-Étienne at Bourges spans the entire Gothic period, just as its tall silhouette dominates the vast horizon of the Berry countryside. 'All Paris is not worth Bourges cathedral,' wrote Balzac in a letter. 'I experienced a curious sensation,' was Stendhal's reaction; 'I was a Christian.' The west front has five doorways opening on

The fortress of Bonaguil. On the borders of Périgord Noir and Quercy, an exceptional example of early sixteenth-century military architecture.

Under the guise of a traditional stronghold it was well adapted to the new advances in artillery, with loopholes for cannon and musket.

(TOP RIGHT) Fifteenth-century frescoes in the chapel of Château de la Verrerie.

(CENTRE RIGHT) Sumptuous decoration in the Salon Doré, Château de Bourdeilles.

(BOTTOM RIGHT) The elegant ribs of the Château de l'Herm.

PALAIS JACQUES-COEUR, BOURGES.

(TOP) *Manoir d'Eyrignac; the plain seventeenth-century house and, in front, its beautiful eighteenth-century gardens.*

(ABOVE LEFT) *Turenne, Corrèze.*

(OPPOSITE) *The east end of the cathedral of St-Étienne, in Bourges, with its stunning flying buttresses and turrets.*

to the nave and four vast aisles; the absence of transepts increases the sense of unity. The difference in elevation of the two-tiered flying buttresses made it possible to build windows in the first tier, whose arches anticipate the soaring vault above the second tier. As a result, five zones of light and shade alternate from top to bottom of the cathedral, creating incomparable perspectives. Stunning stained glass illuminates the choir, once described as 'night lit by sapphires and rubies'. The top of the north tower offers a view of Bourges perched on its hill, surrounded by marshland.

The feudal influence is more marked in Périgord and Auvergne, although the volcanic stone of the Auvergne is better suited to the strictures of classical style than to Renaissance ornament. Elegant houses sprang up at Assier, Hautefort, Puyguilhem and Montal, which was miraculously reconstituted by its new owner at the beginning of this century. The domestic architecture of Sarlat, Riom, Montferrand and Salers also shows the touch of Italianate grace. These houses, castles and manors, gradually opening up to an outside world that was developing a taste for better living, are often located in lush countryside. They give the region a comfortable and prosperous air, prompting the thought that, behind the grey or golden walls and beneath the stone roofs, some tasty local dish must be cooking.

The art of living well

THE HUNT FOR TRUFFLES

THE Germans have a saying, to 'live like God in France'. This could well apply to any number of places in the Bourbonnais, Berry and Limousin, but nowhere is it more apt than in the Périgord.

Every year thousands of visitors come to the Dordogne for a taste of this good life that seems to be imprinted on the landscape. Its gentle appeal lies in the harmony of man and nature. In Périgord Noir, famous for the truffles which grow at the foot of oak trees, the dense green ilex forests are intersected by fertile valleys; the *causses* of Upper Quercy are covered with juniper, oak and the first vines.

The mildness of the climate in Périgord and Quercy suits the most varied types of farming, and the region's great markets at Sarlat, Monpazier, Brive-la-Gaillarde, Lalbenque, Belvès and Villefranche-du-Périgord are full of local produce. Here you can buy *foie gras* or duck and goose conserves, to be eaten with wild mushrooms and garlic potatoes fried in goose fat; other specialities are walnuts and chestnuts, plums, strawberries and sweet grapes. The richly odorous truffles, the 'black diamonds' of the Périgord, are traded discreetly. The little round goat cheeses from Aurillac, Salers and the Margeride plateau are traditionally eaten with salad tossed in walnut oil.

The best-known cheeses – St-Nectaire, Bleu d'Auvergne and Cantal – come from the lush pastures of Cantal and Forez in the Auvergne. Fourme d'Ambert, a blue cheese renowned for its flavour, used to be made by the women on the uplands of Forez. Further to the north, in the Berry, the small village of Chavignol, in the shadow of Sancerre, produces a delicious goat cheese and the crisp white wines that complement it so well.

The vineyards of the Berry, Périgord and Quercy, though less well known than those of Burgundy and Bordeaux, have some pleasant surprises in store. As well as the lighter wines of Sancerre, Menetou-Salon, Reuilly and Valençay, there are the darker, heavier wines of Cahors. The sweet, golden and heady Monbazillac is drunk chilled as an apéritif, with *foie gras* or with dessert, and the dry, fruity white wines of Montravel and Bergerac go well with fish and seafood. Pécharmant is a smooth, full-bodied red; Corent and Châteaugay are produced in the Côtes d'Auvergne; and St-Porçain comes from a little further north. The Auvergne, like the Limousin, is better known for its liqueurs, made from raspberries, walnuts, bilberries, sloes and hazelnuts.

The regions of the Berry, Limousin and Auvergne are rugged: they have a correspondingly simple cuisine, with the emphasis on abundance and quality. Among the delicious local specialities that deserve to be tasted are *potée auvergnate*, a traditional stew full of appetizing ingredients, *tripoux* or tripe dishes from Aurillac, St-Flour and Chaudes-Aigues, *aligot*, a rustic cheese and potato dish from Aubrac, thick soups like *tourain blanchi* from Périgord and *bréjaude* from the Limousin, and *poulet en barbouille*, a chicken stew from the Berry. There are wonderful freshwater fish dishes like trout soufflé or crayfish in cream sauce with wild mushrooms; the local pastries are also excellent.

The regional cooking, which is closely linked to the produce of the earth, makes its own contribution towards the human heritage in these regions.

(LEFT) Tobacco hanging up to dry in the Lot.

(OPPOSITE, TOP LEFT) Fresh vegetables from the Lot.

(OPPOSITE, TOP RIGHT) Stringing garlic bulbs.

(OPPOSITE, BOTTOM LEFT) The truffle market, Lalbenque.

(OPPOSITE, BOTTOM RIGHT) The famous geese of Périgord.

(ABOVE) The pilgrimage town of Rocamadour. The roof tiles of Quercy houses, in their seductively warm colours, display a great variety of shape and pitch.

(LEFT) The beautiful wooden frame of the covered market, Place des Consuls, Martel. Built on a causse in Haut-Quercy, Martel is also called the 'town of seven towers'.

The rural tradition

FEW parts of France have a rural tradition so deeply rooted. Life for those who cultivated the land or practised a craft has, however, never been easy. Many Auvergnats left their homes to sell their produce or their skills, and between 1850 and 1950 half the population of the Creuse emigrated. The folk songs of the Auvergne express the nostalgia for the lost country. For those who remained, adolescence signalled the start of a hard life of labour in an apprenticeship or a trade.

The craft tradition has always provided one of the region's richest resources: coppersmiths from Cantal, cutlers from Thiers, papermakers from Livarot, enamellers from Mozac, stonemasons from Volvic and lacemakers from Le Puy-en-Velay. Their memory is scrupulously preserved in a number of local museums, like the Cutlers' Hall and cutlery museum at Thiers and the Richard de Bas mill in the Lagat valley near Ambert, where paper has been made since the fourteenth century. In the Berry, the traditions of fine craftsmanship were centred on Gargilesse and the village of La Borne near Sancerre, where in the nineteenth century the Talbot family created charming pottery now on display in Berry's provincial museum in the Hôtel Cujas in Bourges.

Modern artists have given these traditions a new lease of life. The centuries-old art of tapestry-making, imported from Flanders, is perpetuated at Aubusson and Felletin in the Creuse. The walls of dozens of castles are still hung with ancient tapestries known as *verdures*, while the famous tapestry of the Lady with the Unicorn at the Cluny Museum, in Paris, is said to have been woven by Aubusson craftsmen. Today there is a new generation of tapestry artists, inspired by the marvellous designs of Jean Lurçat (1892-1966), many of whose works can be seen in the tapestry museum in Aubusson.

The region's memories, however, are expressed not just in these ancient trades; the inhabitants, their houses, legends and beliefs also summon up the past. Making use of local rock, limestone, granite and brick, the domestic architecture fits harmoniously into the landscape. Villages like Salers, Ségur, Meymac, Collonges-la-Rouge, St Léon sur Vézère, Les Arques and La Roque-Gageac, and small towns like Sarlat, St Flour and Uzerche, the 'pearl of Limousin', adorn the countryside. Often they are dominated by a Romanesque church, imposing like Notre-Dame-du-Puy or with the vivid beauty of the churches of Auvergne. Small but perfectly proportioned, these look larger than they really are and have a definite character of their own. The great cathedral of Notre-Dame-du-Port at Clermont-Ferrand is one of the most

(*ABOVE*) *In the heart of Périgord Noir, Sarlat-la-Canéda is a magnificent small town of narrow medieval streets and perfectly restored Gothic and Renaissance houses.*

(*LEFT*) *A handsome residence in La Roque-Gageac, a village of picturesque alleys in a marvellous site on the Dordogne.*

delightful Romanesque churches in France; other examples are at St-Nectaire, Orcival, Issoire, Brioude and St-Saturnin. The churches of the Berry are more modest and sometimes decorated with frescoes, as at Vic, Brinay and Palluau; in the Limousin, distinctive octagonal lantern towers rise proudly into the sky. There are countless such sanctuaries, densely surrounded by houses, to be discovered by chance throughout the region.

Every seven years in the villages of the Limousin effigies of patron saints are borne through the streets in solemn procession, providing an occasion for colourful parades. In Auvergne, the cult of the Virgin is celebrated in numerous processions and pilgrimages; effigies of the Virgin, which include some of the oldest in France, are striking for their hieratic pose and the realism of their peasant faces.

The deeper aspects of the region's character are still marked by ancient superstitions, haloed by legends in which spells and sorcerers coexist with the cult of saints. Witches are everywhere in the Berry, as George Sand related in a collection of country tales. In the Creuse, the nights are peopled by hellish washerwomen, werewolves and a 'cursed ox'. Bourges has become the capital of alchemists because of the arcane symbols remaining in the Palais Jacques Coeur and the Hôtel Lallemant. Sabbaths are still said to take place at full moon on the mysterious heights of the Monts de Blond. The Church, for all its stone crosses and wayside chapels, has never managed to root out the old pagan beliefs. The church towers, 'lanterns of the dead', seem to be the link between these two worlds, reconciling the sign of the cross with the pagan idea of the return of the dead to the light.

In spite of respect for a rural past, a living folklore and a dialect which, though less often spoken nowadays, is still very well understood, modern communications have strengthened the region's central position as a crossroads. Agriculture and industry flourish, and famous festivals attracting crowds of visitors keep the cultural traditions alive. The Limousin has become a focal point of contemporary art, with displays and exhibitions in centres at Vassivière, Meymac, Rochechouart and Limoges, the centre of the porcelain industry.

Holidays in the region are a combination of pleasure and discovery. To make the most of them the visitor must enter into local life, visit the markets and, above all, succumb to the call of the wide open spaces.

(TOP LEFT) Effigy of the Black Virgin at Le Puy-en-Velay.

(BOTTOM LEFT) The Virgin enthroned in the Romanesque church at Orcival.

(RIGHT) Besse-en-Chandesse, in the Auvergne.

RUE
NOTRE-DAME

RUE DE LA
BOUCHERIE

Vitality and health

AUVERGNE VIEWED FROM THE SKY.

A few hours' drive from many of the major French cities, the Massif Central is an ideal place for outdoor activities. The only thing missing is the sea, but numerous rivers, dams and lakes cater for devotees of water sports.

There is water everywhere, from the falls at Gimel to the innumerable streams that have their source on the slopes of the Massif, offering all types of fishing, opening out into vast reservoirs behind dams, breaking up into a myriad of small lakes and ponds, or welling up in soothing springs after a long journey underground.

One of the most striking features of the Auvergne is the number of mineral and thermal springs along the fault lines of the volcanic region. The Puy-de-Dôme *département* and the Vichy basin alone account for one third of all the springs in France. The thermal springs have their origins in the fragile zones of the earth's crust, on the fault lines that frame the rift valley of the Limagne or within volcanic regions. Their therapeutic qualities are many and varied: people go to Vichy, the 'queen of spas', for the digestion, Royat for the heart and arteries, Châtel-Guyon for the intestine, Mont-Dore for asthma and respiratory ailments, Bourboule for the respiratory tract and lymphatic system, St-Nectaire for the kidneys, Bourbon-l'Archambault for rheumatism and broken bones, Néris-les-Bains for nervous complaints, Chaudes-Aigues and Châteauneuf-les-Bains for rheumatism. In season, these charming spa towns exude an atmosphere of elegance; the baths themselves, splendid architectural reminders of the Belle Époque, are now equipped with the most up-to-date facilities. New health centres and luxury hotels have sprung up, with spacious parks surrounding them. As cures take up only part of a day, there is a vast array of sports, entertainments and excursions on offer which attract large numbers of visitors.

Many of these resorts make ideal bases for walks, especially in the regional parks. These nature reserves make wonderful places to see traditional activities and wildlife conservation being pursued alongside modern economic developments. Most of them have visitor information centres providing information on local wildlife and crafts.

In the Auvergne volcano park, the largest wildlife park in France, walkers can commune undisturbed with nature between the *puys*, the Sancy, the vast grasslands of the Cézallier, the granite scree of Artense and the moorlands, lakes and peat bogs. In the Livradois-Forez regional park, visitors can discover the countryside around La Chaise-Dieu and the Black Woods and the secretive patchwork of lakes around the Brenne, where birds of prey perch by the roadside, plovers run in watermeadows and herons take wing from reed beds. There are any number of walks you can take: for instance, from Ségur to Pompadour, perhaps catching a horse race in the town where the first Anglo-Arab horses were bred; over Gramat *causse*; up the hill to Rochechouart, with a fine view from the castle; along the wooded banks of the Bouriane or the Creuse; in the Ambazac hills or the peat-bogs of Longéroux, near Meymac.

There are also opportunities for bicycle rides through the woodland around Nohant and La Châtre, on the Millevaches plateau, along the Cher, through the gently undulating

(*ABOVE*) *Three-hundred-year-old oaks are the glory of the Forêt de Tronçais, one of the finest forests in France.*

(*OPPOSITE*) *Halle des Sources, Vichy. Vichy's carbonated waters have been appreciated since Roman times.*

countryside of the Bourbonnais and in the majestic forests of Châteauroux and Tronçais.

Lakes such as Vassivière and Bort are ideal for water sports, swimming and fishing. You can canoe or kayak down the Dordogne or Vézère and see some unforgettable views of cliffs and castles. You can take to the air in micro-lights, hang-gliders, balloons and gliders or descend into the bowels of the earth in the caves and potholes of the Lot and Dordogne. In winter, the main sport is skiing, cross-country on the Limousin uplands and at Sancy, Cantal and Velay, downhill in the Puy-de-Dôme and Cantal with major resorts like Mont Dore, Super-Besse and Super-Lioran.

For those in search of culture, there is the spring music festival in Bourges, which attracts many well-known musicians and often discovers new talents. The magnificent old abbey church of La Chaise-Dieu rings to the rafters with music during the summer festival. Confolens has an international folk festival, Clermont-Ferrand a short film festival, Murat a comic-strip festival, Sarlat a theatre festival, St-Céré a music and opera festival, Limoges a festival of the French-speaking world, Nohant a festival of romantic art, literature and music and Noirlac a summer arts festival.

The centre of France exerts an undeniable appeal. It is a favourite holiday destination all the year round and visitors leave feeling refreshed, with their equilibrium restored.

At a time when communications were much more difficult than they are today, writers like George Sand, Alain Fournier, Jean Giraudoux, Marcel Jonhandeau and Claude Michelet, who all spent part of their lives in these regions, kept faithfully returning. The local literature is astonishingly rich: it describes the spirit of the land and its wily, spontaneous and hardy people. Whereas for centuries life in these regions was poor and arduous, today there are all sorts of hidden treasures for the visitor to discover.

The Atlantic Coast

The Atlantic and its mild climate give a harmony to south-west France, otherwise famous for its vineyards. To the south, the chain of the Pyrenees rises to peaks more than 2,000 metres high.

FISHING IN THE MARAIS POITEVIN.

THE Atlantic coastline, stretching from the south of Brittany to the Spanish border, contains havens of spectacular emptiness and beauty. Away from the bustling urban centres, the coast and its hinterland offer a landscape of startling contrasts, from immense beaches, dunes, mud-flats and marshes to plains, hills, pine forests and woodlands. Wherever you are, the ocean seems omnipresent; whipped up by angry storms or reflecting the fiery rays of sunset, it changes perpetually with the mood of the sky. For fishermen, salt-workers and traders, this long strip of shoreline hugging the land between the Loire and the Pyrenees has always been a profitable source of income.

At every step, the countryside stirs an emotion or a memory of the past. The Marais Poitevin, the network of waterways first created by medieval monks along the banks of the Sèvre Niortaise river, are best navigated by boat, when the marshlands unfold as a kind of enchanted fairyland. On the edge of the marsh stands the majestic Maillezais Abbey, its mystery preserved through the ages. Developed as a naval base against the English, the severe seventeenth-century port of Rochefort spreads out beside its arsenal and rope factory, the superb Corderie Royale, reminders of the town's military and mercantile past. To the east, Poitiers provides a rare choice of monuments for lovers of art and architecture .

Near the mouth of the Garonne estuary, the Romanesque church of Talmont perches attractively on a cliff above the pounding waters of the Gironde. As the eye travels across the splendid panorama to the south, it soon catches sight of the prestigious vineyards of the Bordelais region. Here are names to conjure with – Médoc, Haut-Médoc, Blaye, St Émilion and Graves. Nowhere on earth is more perfectly suited to the aristocratic art of wine making than this hundred or so square kilometres of vineyards and châteaux. A little farther south, fringed by pinewoods, the natural indentations of the Arcachon basin and the extraordinary dune of Pilat bear witness to the perpetual battle between land and sea.

Venturing inland, the visitor is beguiled by the charms of the fertile Lot Valley and the mild climate of the Garonne. In the Gers district, after admiring some of the outstanding *bastides* – the fortified villages of south-west Gascony –

gourmets face the tantalizing choice between the gastronomic delights of *foie gras, magret de canard* or *ortolans aux confits*.

Once inland, at the foot of the Pyrenees, it is difficult to imagine that the sea is only a short distance away. Yet this continuous 400-kilometre mountain barrier is the link between the Mediterranean and the Atlantic, where the Bidassoa river has marked the border between France and Spain since the Treaty of the Pyrenees was signed between the two countries in 1659.

(OPPOSITE, TOP) Stilt houses of the Arcachon basin, a vast triangular bay almost closed off by the narrow strip of land of the Cap-Ferret.

(OPPOSITE, CENTRE) Château de Pichon-Longueville, Haut-Médoc.

(OPPOSITE, BOTTOM) The wine store, responsibility of the maître de chai, *Château Margaux.*

(ABOVE) Valley of the river Bidassoa, which forms the frontier between France and Spain in the Pays Basque.

Ocean life

COASTAL FISHING ALONG
THE ATLANTIC SHORE.

AFICIONADOS of the Atlantic will say that the coast is at its most beautiful at high tide – when the estuaries fill up, and the swelling waves crash against rocks and cliffs and stretch out in long parallel crests across the dunes. At low tide the spectacle loses some of its force: the shore lies exposed, strewn with seaweed and other flotsam, while at river mouths mere trickles of water wind their way through the silt.

From the Pays de Retz to the foot of the Pyrenees, the surf's ceaseless ebb and flow punctuates the seasons: in high summer, holidaymakers bathe in the sea or boat on rivers while children play on the strand; in the depths of winter there are long walks beside the water's edge. But here, as on coasts everywhere, the shoreline is constantly changing. Since the beginning of time, it has been continually transformed by the effect of the sea, the tides and the coastal currents.

As well as regulating the pattern of life on the coast, the sea also governs maritime activities in the ports throughout the year. From the quays of La Rochelle, Les Sables d'Olonne and St-Gilles trawlers leave for long deep-sea fishing expeditions in the Bay of Biscay. Tuna, sardines and anchovies have made the reputation of the fishermen of St-Jean-de-Luz. Lobsters and crayfish are caught in the cold waters off the rocky coasts of the Vendée, and prawns are a speciality of Royan. Many fishermen make a living supplying varieties of freshly caught fish and seafood for a connoisseur's market. All kinds of fishing and angling, with line, rope and nets, are practised along the coast and inshore.

Over the centuries the ocean has sculpted and hollowed the shoreline, leaving cliff faces and vast stretches of fine sand. Here and there it has caused odd formations such as the Virgin's Rock at Biarritz and the narrow inlet at La Rochelle in which the old fortified harbour nestles.

Together, geology and the sea have also produced a string of small islands off the Vendée and Charente Maritime coasts. In these peaceful spots, where time seems to stand still, you can sit and contemplate the silence while gazing at the horizon. Each island has its own identity: Yeu with its wild rocky coastline, Noirmoutier whose light so impressed Auguste Renoir, Ré with its small white cottages and salt-marshes, Aix, fortified by Vauban in 1699 and home to Napoleon during his last days in France, and the largest of them all, Oléron, with its particularly mild climate.

(TOP) Oyster beds in the Arcachon basin, one of the great oyster-growing centres of Europe.

(ABOVE) Salt-marsh workers, Noirmoutier.

(OPPOSITE) Fishing in the Gironde; in winter the catch is lamprey and shad, in spring baby eel.

The appeal of Bordeaux, the great
city of the south-west on the
Garonne, is its splendid
eighteenth-century buildings and
its lively centre.

(ABOVE) A public garden.

(RIGHT) The east end of St-André
Cathedral, seen from the Tour Pey
Berland; in the background, the
eighteenth-century façade of the
Hôtel de Ville and the Mériadeck
district.

(OPPOSITE, TOP) Interior of the
Grand Théâtre, built by Victor
Louis in 1780. From the painted
ceiling hangs a chandelier made
from 14,000 Bohemian crystals.

(OPPOSITE, BELOW LEFT) Pont
de Pierre, completed in 1822.

(OPPOSITE, BELOW RIGHT)
Place de la Bourse, laid out in the
eighteenth century.

Eighteenth-century Bordeaux

'TAKE Versailles, add Antwerp, and you have Bordeaux,' was how Victor Hugo described this impressive city on its splendid tidal river, the Garonne. The history of Bordeaux goes back to the Middle Ages when it was under English rule. It was the English who were responsible for introducing its people to seafaring and for turning the town into an important trading port through the export of its wines. Throughout the fifteenth century, the troubles of the Hundred Years War failed to put a stop to this trade in 'claret', the word adopted by the English from the old French *clairet,* and up until the seventeenth century, its export was an annual event, safeguarded by English and Dutch vessels. In the eighteenth century, colonial goods from the West Indies added to the traffic, further stimulating the development of this great port and establishing Bordeaux as one of the richest towns in provincial France.

One of the most important historical events for the destiny of France took place in 1137, when Eleanor, only daughter of William, duke of Aquitaine, married the future Louis VII of France: she came with a dowry consisting of nearly the whole of south-western France. This marriage proved to be a failure and ended in divorce fifteen years later.

Several weeks later, Eleanor married Henry Plantagenet, duke of Normandy, count of Anjou, ruler of Touraine and Maine; their combined territories covered an area which was even more vast than that ruled by the king of France. Ironically, however, Henry's succession to the English throne as Henry II in 1154 was a political disaster for the Capet monarchy; the conflict it heralded between England and France was to last three centuries.

Today, Bordeaux remains a prosperous centre with some magnificent eighteenth-century monuments, including the Grand Théâtre, one of the most beautiful theatres in France. Built between 1773 and 1780 by Victor Louis in the Louis XVI style, it predates Ledoux's theatre in Besançon and Vailly's

(ABOVE) *Cours Xavier-Arnozan, in the Chartrons district.*

(RIGHT) *Doors and knockers, in Bordeaux of yesterday and today.*

(OPPOSITE) *Fountain of the monument to the Girondins on the Esplanade des Quinconces.*

FAÇADE OF THE PLACE DU
PARLEMENT.

Odéon in Paris. Massive in scale, dramatic in character but restrained in decoration, the architecture of the Grand Théâtre was a triumph of innovation inspired by the buildings of Antiquity.

Bordeaux stands at the first bridging point of the Garonne, some 98 kilometres from the coast. The mainstream of life takes place in the city's heart, where locals gather in the famous squares, around the large open Esplanade des Quinconces, surrounded by its elegant buildings, in the Place de la Bourse and the Place du Parlement. Les Chartrons, a district behind the Quayside made fashionable by Bordeaux high society who built their town houses here, also has some fine eighteenth-century houses with classical façades.

The prestige of this city derives not just from its monumental architecture and rich history, but also from the important artistic and cultural events that it hosts. The performances, recitals and concerts at the annual May festival, for example, attract amateur musicians and dancers from all over the world.

A backward glance

As the former capital of Guyenne (the old English corruption of 'Aquitaine'), Bordeaux has played a determining role in the history of France. Here the Black Prince established his court; Cardinal Richelieu, Louis XIII's first minister, set up the system of Intendants, the first local administrators of the crown; and during the French Revolution, the federalist Girondins' party was formed from Bordeaux deputies.

It is not, however, the only place in south-west France to have been marked by history. One of the bloodiest events was the war between the 'Whites' (royalists) and the 'Blues' (republicans) in the Vendée following the Revolution of 1793. This *bocage* countryside, controlled by the royalist Catholic troops, rose up against the excesses of the Convention. One

(TOP) Capital in the choir of the church of St-Pierre, Chauvigny.

(ABOVE) Torch procession, Lourdes.

(RIGHT) Cloister of the abbey, Nieul-sur-l'Autise.

(OPPOSITE) St-Hilaire-le-Grand, Poitiers.

year later, thousands of 'Whites' were executed by General Turreau's army and the countryside was devastated. This was the worst episode in this tragic three-year civil war. The history of the uprising is commemorated in the museum of La Maison de La Chabotterie, near La Roche-sur-Yon.

Pau, the elegant capital of Béarn in the Pyrenees, was the birthplace of Henri IV, whose Edict of Nantes ended the wars of religion in 1598. On his accession, he had proclaimed himself 'King of France and Navarre' and, deferring to the independent spirit of the Bearnais people, announced, 'I give France to Béarn, not Béarn to France'. In the reign of his son Louis XIII, this ancient province was annexed to the French crown, although it remained a *pays d'états* until the Revolution.

At St-Jean-de-Luz in 1660, Louis XIV married the Spanish Infanta, María Teresa of Austria, with enormous pomp and ceremony followed by lavish festivities and entertainments. In the previous year France and Spain had signed the Treaty of the Pyrenees on an island in the Bidassoa river, near the border town of Hendaye.

Architectural splendour

Bordeaux, Poitiers and Saintes were all in turn the capital of the Roman colony of Aquitaine. Many Gallo-Roman remains have survived, in spite of vandalism in the nineteenth century. Among them are the ruins of amphitheatres (Saintes), theatres (Les Bouchauds, Vieux-Poitiers), temples and bath-houses

(Sanxay), and votive arches (Saintes), all of which give us a good understanding of the principal characteristics of Gallo-Roman civilization.

The early Middle Ages were marked by conflicts between the great feudal families. The eleventh century, however, saw a renewal of faith exemplified in the Crusades and the great pilgrimages. In the south-west of France many important churches sprang up along the pilgrim route to the tomb of St James at Santiago de Compostela in Spain. This meeting point for pilgrims from all over Europe soon became as famous as Jerusalem and Rome.

Romanesque architecture spread throughout France during the eleventh and twelfth centuries, with several stylistic differences depending on the region and the period. In Poitou and Saintonge, the originality of the churches lay in the height of the side aisles, which served to reinforce the central nave and buttress and to balance the barrel vaulting. The west front was usually characterized by abundant arcading with statues and low reliefs. In Poitiers, where the major monuments date from this period, the church of Notre-Dame-la-Grande is a fine example of Poitevin Romanesque. The sumptuous decoration and rich carving on the twelfth-century façade make it one of the most famous churches in France.

At this time, the south-west, and in particular the former region of Aquitaine – the subject of rival claims by the French and English for three centuries – was scattered with fortresses,

some little more than crude strongholds. These were followed by brick castles and remarkable fortified churches which acted as refuges for local populations. Throughout the thirteenth century, however, architecture in Aquitaine was dominated by the *bastide*, a part-rural, part-urban 'new town'. In Gascony and Guyenne the *bastides* were so dense – between Périgord and the Pyrenees they number about three hundred – that they were probably the most important form of collective habitation in the region. As these fortified towns proliferated, many new churches were built. In Gascony they share similarities, with

belfry-porches (Mirande, Marciac) and wide, dark naves lit mainly through the clerestory windows of a cramped apse.

The late eighteenth-century Louis XVI style of architecture was popular not only in Bordeaux but throughout the Bordelais countryside. One example is the *chartreuse,* the small, graceful château or manor house typical of the Guyenne region, especially around the vineyards of Bordeaux. Low-built, usually without an upper storey, and opening directly on to a terrace or flower garden, *chartreuses* were the local aristocracy's country retreats.

The Landes

(OPPOSITE) *An arcaded Gascony house, Mauvezin.*

(RIGHT) *The great forest at the heart of the Landes regional nature park of Gascony.*

(BELOW) *Landes bullfights are the most appreciated in Gascony. The écarteur has to jump out the way of the bull's head; there is no death.*

RUNNING parallel to the ocean from north to south, from the Gironde to the Adour rivers, the Landes is a huge area of reclaimed land bordering the ruler-straight shoreline of the Côte d'Argent, where the only indentation is that of the Arcachon basin. Since the successful draining of the dunes in the nineteenth century, it has become one immense commercial pine forest. The mainly flat countryside is, nevertheless, a wonderful place for ramblers and for those seeking peace and quiet. The Landes regional park, where the fresh scent of pines mingles with the salt smell of the sea, is famous for its exceptionally healthy climate. Picturesque local houses, usually sited in clearings, are typically half-timbered with dormer windows, gables and light rough-cast walls.

On the edge of the Gironde Landes in the north, the austere lines of the fifteenth-century Château de La Brède are mirrored in three large moats. The birthplace of the eighteenth-century philosopher Montesquieu, this property, in the Pays des Graves, remains largely unchanged from the time when he used to come here to enjoy its peace and quiet. Montesquieu, who began his career as a Bordeaux magistrate, had a passionate love of travelling, of the countryside and of his vineyard. At this austere, almost mystic castle, he wrote *The Spirit of the Law*, the political treatise which set out his theory of the separation of legislative, executive and judicial powers, the sole guarantee of civil liberties.

[199]

The Pays Basque

After the dunes and wide open spaces of the Landes plain, the Pays Basque comes as a surprise. The mountains suddenly seem very close, and the coast, with its jagged cliffs and rocks, is a complete contrast to the Landes shoreline, which stretches out straight as a die. The hinterland, with its lush green valleys and typically whitewashed houses, seems to belong to a totally different world.

Strange as it may seem, the origin of the Basque people and of their language remains an enigma. The Basques have a distinct identity and are fiercely attached to tradition. They give pride of place in their lives to the church, just as much as to folklore and the famous sport of *pelota* or *chistera*. Every tournament becomes an event at which natives and tourists draw together in the warmth of the festive atmosphere. The game is played with six players, three a side. The *pelota*, which is larger than a tennis ball, is hurled against the high *fronton* wall and returned by the opponent either at full pitch or after it has bounced once within the limits marked on the ground.

(TOP) *Making the basket-weave* chistera, *for the game of that name, derived from the characteristic 'gutter' or channel.*

(ABOVE) *Ringside spectators.*

(RIGHT) *Grand Chistera, the Basque game of* pelota.

(OPPOSITE, TOP) *The beaches of the Basque and Landes coasts are a surfer's paradise.*

(OPPOSITE, BOTTOM) *Tug-of-war* (sokatira), *a traditional test of strength in the Pays Basque. The finalists face each other in the summer festival at St-Palais.*

(*OPPOSITE*) *Hôtel du Palais, Biarritz. The emperor Napoleon III built the Villa Eugénie, which was later turned into a hotel. Both Queen Victoria and Edward VII came for long stays in Biarritz.*

(*ABOVE AND LEFT*) *Beach life.*

The jewel of the Basque coast, and without doubt of the whole Atlantic coast, is Biarritz. This seaside resort, with its splendid beaches, promenades and gardens, has enjoyed a reputation for luxury since the Spanish nobility discovered its charms in the nineteenth century. The finest example of Biarritz's former glory is the Villa Eugénie, which was built by Napoleon III for his wife, the Empress Eugénie, at the heart of the town. Now transformed into the Hôtel du Palais, it is one of the most beautiful hotels in France and attracts clients from all over the world. The shape of the seabed in this part of the Bay of Biscay and the slope of the beaches produce fine Atlantic rollers, the surfers' delight.

The Pyrenees

ABOVE the hills of the Pays Béarn, the chain of the Pyrenees rises in a seemingly endless series of finely serrated crests. In the Central Pyrenees, the peaks of the Midi d'Ossau and Midi de Bigorre often serve as a backdrop to a multitude of spas and thermal stations. These take advantage of the region's abundant supply of mineral and hot springs, with diverse therapeutic properties, as well as the exceptionally temperate local climate.

Of all the valleys that make up the Pyrenean chain, Cauterets is certainly one of the most picturesque. Bejewelled with lakes and criss-crossed by torrents and limpid mountain streams, it illustrates the traditional Pyrenean charms that have inspired all kinds of artistic talent and entered many a sensitive soul. The originality of the local customs and the exoticism of nearby Spain appeal to the romantic taste of many people and add to the resort's attractions.

The splendid glacial Cirque de Gavarnie, set at the upper end of a blind valley in the Central Pyrenees, is also a remarkable beauty spot. This great natural amphitheatre, often described as 'the end of the world', has always excited the imaginative spirit. In an almost unreal setting, its waterfalls, canyons, gorges and forests make for an unforgettable scenic experience which is both grand and impressive.

The Pyrenees offer generous opportunities for all sorts of leisure activities, particularly rambling, mountain climbing and skiing. In winter, the slopes of La Mongie, Cauterets and

(OPPOSITE, TOP) *Pyrenean chamois.*

(OPPOSITE, BOTTOM) *The twelfth-century church tower of the Templars' chapel, Aragnouet.*

(ABOVE) *The circle of jagged mountain summits around Lescun.*

(LEFT) *Pic du Midi d'Ossau, reaching a height of 2,884 metres.*

Superbagnères are popular with skiers who come from Bordeaux, Poitiers and Toulouse.

In spite of all their up-to-date amenities, however, it should not be forgotten that the Pyrenees are of ancient geological formation. Over the course of a million years, the glaciers and giant ice-floes advancing and retreating across the mountain landscape have left their mark. Studies of the area have now established a sound chronology for both human and geological science, making the Pyrenees one of the most interesting areas on earth for research into the prehistory of man. Among the important local finds are the remains of Tautavel man, one of the most ancient species of *homo erectus* outside Africa, who lived here some 450,000 years ago.

Food and wine of distinction

WHILE the rich pastures of Poitou and Charentes produce the most succulent beef, mutton and poultry, the coastal region offers a varied choice of fish from the sea. In Arcachon and in the harbour at Les Sables d'Olonne generous portions of seafood are served in restaurants at all hours of the day. *Mouclade charentaise*, mussels cooked in the *marinière* fashion with a delicious wine sauce, is definitely a dish to look out for. The extraordinary variety of shellfish along the coast is a challenge to any appetite. There are lobsters, crayfish, prawns, crabs, mussels and shrimps, to mention some of them, not forgetting the Marennes-Oléron oysters which are fattened in pools known as *claires,* and eaten either plain or accompanied by tiny hot sausages or slices of pâté.

It is when approaching the south-west of France that the word gastronomy takes on its full meaning. The home of culinary art is the land between the rivers of the Garonne and those of the Dordogne, the country that stretches from the mouth of the Gironde to that of the Bidassoa, the Gers valley and the hospitable Gascony. The gastronomy reflects the character of each province, whose reputation it helps to maintain. The cooking around Bordeaux, based on fish and often served with a wine sauce, acts as a good introduction to the cuisine of the Pays Basque: here food is strongly spiced and seasoned, like *piperade*, an omelette with green chilli peppers and tomatoes. It is, however, the specialities of Gascony and the Pays Béarn that are worth going out of your way for. The abundance, variety and quality of the raw materials found in these regions have also attracted many famous chefs, who have finished their culinary training with a spell in the south-west.

The basic ingredients of this rich and delicious cuisine are lard and goose fat, particularly in *confits, salmis* and *magrets.* The most sophisticated of all the specialities of this region, however, are goose and duck livers. One taste and you will understand why the maize fields stretch as far as the eye can see. The bargaining for poultry livers in the boisterous, colourful markets of Gers and Landes, and around Ste-Catherine, is a sight not to be missed. Where else could you

find the legendary *poule-au-pot,* the favourite dish of Henri IV, born in Pau?

The pleasures of the table would, however, be nothing without the wines and spirits to accompany them. Médoc, Margaux, Graves, St Émilion and Pomerol are just a few of the magical names of the great Bordeaux reds to be drunk on special occasions or found on wine lists in the best restaurants. Equally distinguished white wines range from the dry, clean-tasting, vigorous Graves to the great sweet wines of Sauternes, pressed from grapes just beginning to feel the effects of the 'noble rot'.

Lovers of spirits will find brandy of the highest quality in Cognac, the peaceful birthplace of François I that has given its name to the world-famous spirit. There are several different types of cognac, depending upon the amount of time it has spent maturing in porous oak casks from the Limoges district. Armagnac is produced in vineyards which stretch almost throughout the entire Gers district and run into the Landes, Lot and Garonne. A delight for discerning palates, this brandy

is matured in dark, resinous oak casks until it reaches full richness at 42°C, after which it is bottled.

The Atlantic coastline is a world apart. It has something to offer to all the senses: sea and sun, an eventful history, famous inhabitants, architectural masterpieces, wonderful produce and exceptional wines. From the south of the Loire to the Bay of Biscay, the variety and grandeur of the landscape sets off the individual character of each beach, village and valley, giving the visitor a journey out of time.

Nevertheless, the coast and the hinterland have always managed to keep abreast of the times by uniting the great natural beauty of the region to the latest, ultra-sophisticated technology. This is particularly the case in Poitiers, which is host to Futuroscope, a vast complex designed to introduce the public to the latest technology and to heighten their awareness of a society dominated by the image. The numerous attractions on offer, some of which are comparable to those in the Parc de La Villette in Paris, are aimed at those who are curious to discover what the future may hold.

(OPPOSITE) Portico on the façade of Château Margaux.

(RIGHT) Entrance to the wine-cellars of Château Margaux.

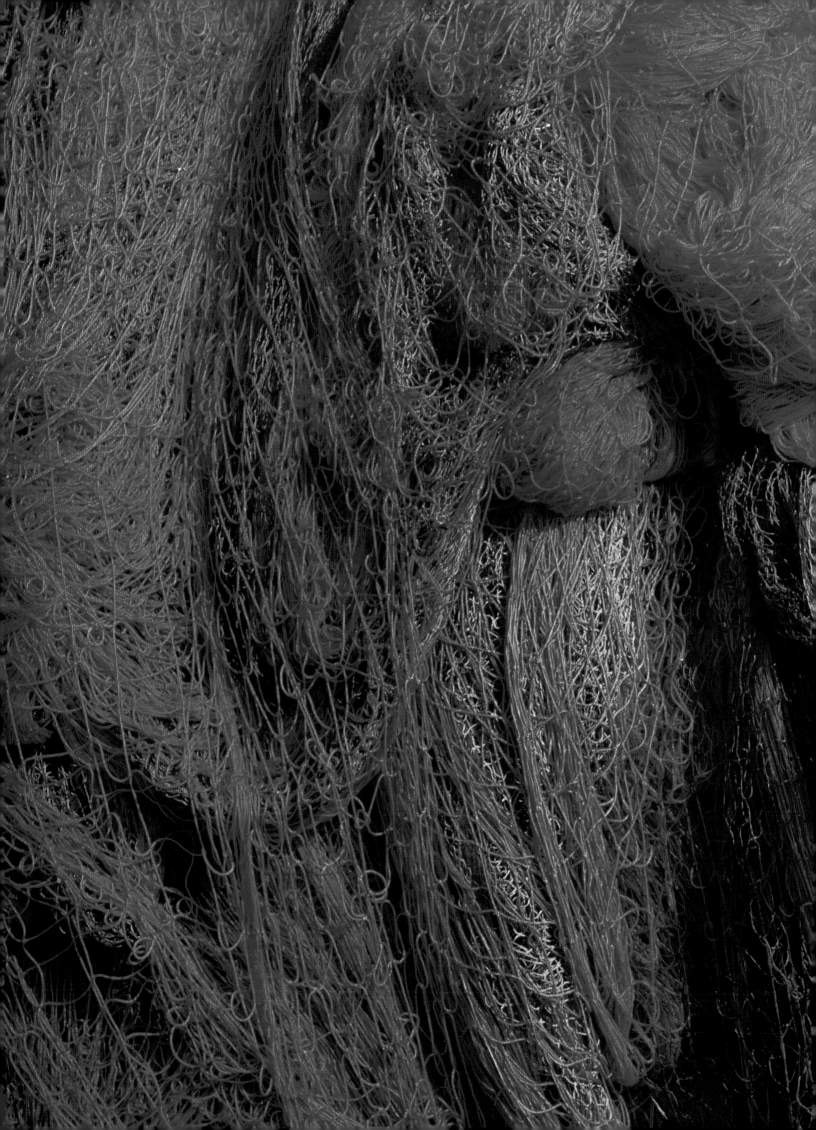

Languedoc and Midi-Pyrenees

A region where the joy of living finds expression in carnivals, markets and rugby matches.

Causes, canyons, and crests

STREET IN ST-GUILHEM-LE-DÉSERT.

BETWEEN the Massif Central, the Rhône, the Mediterranean, the Pyrenees and Périgord is an area divided into small regions and linked only by the old Provençal language, the *langue d'oc*. The mountains of the Aubrac stretch into the Auvergne, the Mediterranean *garrigue* around Nîmes blooms with the flowers of Provence, the Roussillon has its Catalan equivalent across the Spanish border, and the *foie gras* and *confits* produced around Toulouse herald the south-west. Nevertheless, the Languedoc soul is expressed in the *causses*, the Cévennes, on the coast, in the vineyards and in the *garrigue* scrubland.

The *causses* uplands provide some of the grandest landscapes in France. Like the Colorado in the United States, the Tarn, Jonte and Dourbie rivers have hollowed out deep canyons with sheer white limestone sides streaked, through the years, with black and ochre. The gorges, like fresh green oases, divide up the Grands Causses. The vast, arid tablelands of the Sauveterre, Méjean, Noir and Larzac *causses* are dotted with weathered rock formations resembling ghost towns. Where water has seeped into the fissured limestone, it has created extraordinary caves, chasms and swallow-holes, such as the lace-like formations of the Grotte des Demoiselles, the eerie stalagmites of the immense Aven Armand, and the pink chamber of the Grotte de Dargilan. Local dry-stone hamlets blend into the countryside. The long, vaulted sheep-pens shelter flocks of ewes reared for milk to make the famous Roquefort which is matured slowly in underground caves. Rising out of the lonely, rocky Larzac *causse* are the ramparts of twelfth-century settlements belonging to the Knights Templar: Ste-Eulalie-de-Cernon and La Couvertoirade.

To the north-east of the *causses* region are the Cévennes, forming a succession of lowering granite summits between which the shale crests and the narrow valleys of chestnut trees have long been impenetrable. Tall, shale buildings, *magnaneries*, once used for breeding silkworms, are reminders of the days when Lyon merchants came to buy the precious material. This profoundly Protestant region still has a certain austerity.

(LEFT) A hamlet near Le Vigan, Cévennes.

(TOP RIGHT) A flock of sheep on the Méjean causse.

(RIGHT) St-Véran, in the gorges of the Doubie.

Mountains, scrubland and vineyards

THE Massif Central tapers off towards the Pyrenees in a series of smaller massifs: the Monts de l'Espinouse with the gentle, wooded slopes of Mont Somail and the tortured relief of Mont Caroux, the Sidobre plateau with its spectacular jumbles of granite rock and, at the extreme south-west, the Montagne Noire which owes its name to the dark forests that cover its northern slope. From the southern side of the Massif Central there are magnificent views of the Pyrenees, dominated by Mont Canigou, and in the foreground the perfect walled city of Carcassonne looking exactly like an illustration of medieval fortifications out of a children's book.

Farther south, one enters *garrigue* territory. This stretch of arid scrubland grazed by sheep, between the Rhône and the Aude rivers, the sea and the mountains, is what gives the Midi-Pyrenees its identity. A striking landscape demonstrating the marriage between dry white limestone and scrubby vegetation, the *garrigue* is covered by tiny evergreen oaks, cistus shrubs, junipers and herbs such as rosemary, thyme, basil and mint that scent the surrounding countryside.

Gaillac, Minervois, Rivesaltes, Limoux, Banyuls, Frontignan and Corbières are the evocative names of local wines. The vineyards on large estates around Béziers surround the châteaux built at the turn of the century. In the Roussillon, Corbières and Fenouillèdes, the vines clinging to the slopes form small pockets of greenery in the harsh, dry landscape. The history of Languedoc and Roussillon is linked to its wine industry, the main economic activity of the region. The uprising in 1907 by small wine growers against the Clemenceau government is still remembered in the annals of local history.

(BELOW AND OPPOSITE ABOVE) The ramparts of Carcassonne.

(*OPPOSITE, RIGHT*) *Field of sunflowers and dovecote with its flight-platform in the Tarn.*

(*FAR LEFT*) *Detail of a door, Pays Catalan.*

(*LEFT*) *Sculptured heads decorating the wooden arcading in the market square of the bastide of Mirepoix, near Toulouse.*

UNTIL relatively recently, the coastline, consisting of flat marshes, lagoons and endless sandy beaches, remained a tourist developer's dream. For decades, the only seaside resort was Palavas-les-Flots, a sort of French Clacton-on-Sea at which families from Montpellier, armed with buckets, spades and shrimping nets, would arrive on Sundays on the small train immortalized in cartoons by Dubout. The rest of the coast was totally inhospitable because of the danger of malaria from the mosquito-infested lagoons.

In the 1960s, the development of the Languedoc-Roussillon coast was finally approved. It began with a titanic drainage effort followed by the construction of tourist units whose names today are well known: La Grande Motte, Cap d'Agde, Leucate and Gruissan. The area was transformed with Florida-style resorts, whose apartments and marinas quickly drew large crowds of holidaymakers who came to enjoy the sun and sea on the sandy beaches.

At the centre of this coast and one of its oldest communities, Sète, standing alone on its peninsula overlooking the Thau lagoon, has preserved its character as a fishing harbour: it is the most important on the Mediterranean coast. Two of its famous sons have sung its praises: Paul Valéry in his poem *Le Cimitière Marin* and the singer Georges Brassens in his song, *Supplique pour être enterré sur la plage de Sète* ('Oh to be buried on the beach at Sète'). Another singer, Charles Trenet, a native of Narbonne, has also written songs about the charming inlets on the Côte Vermeille (vermilion coast), south of Perpignan.

Huddled in bays along this stretch of coast, at the foot of the vineyard-covered slopes of the Pyrenees, are the harbours of Banyuls, Port-Vendres and Collioure, one of the favourite spots of the artists of the Fauve School. Here, Matisse, Derain and Braque would set up their easels on the Boromar beach to paint the Château Royal, built by the kings of Majorca, and the church of Notre-Dame-des-Anges reflected in the bright blue water. The Côte Vermeille leads into the Catalan Costa Brava; from Cadaqués, a short distance away, Salvador Dali would come to admire the station at Perpignan, which he described as the 'centre of the universe'.

(OPPOSITE, TOP) Les Toits de Collioure, *by Matisse, 1905.*

(FAR LEFT) Repairing the nets at Sète.

(LEFT) The sardana, *Catalan dance.*

(TOP RIGHT) Harbour of Collioure and the church tower of Notre-Dame-des-Anges.

(RIGHT) Thau lagoon, Mèze.

A rich artistic heritage

THE presence of early man in the Pyrenees and the Roussillon can be traced back some 450,000 years. About 300,000 years after Tautavel man, Neanderthal man was chasing bears and reindeer. Then, about 14,000 years ago, our direct *homo sapiens* ancestors were drawing outstanding figures of bison, stags and horses in the Grotte de Niaux. The Mas-d'Azil cave points to a further milestone in the evolution of mankind: mysterious painted pebbles discovered there could be either early lunar calendars or the beginnings of abstract numbering.

More recently, in the Bronze Age, the *causses* and Cévennes were dotted with megaliths in the form of dolmens, menhirs and covered alleyways. The most outstanding examples are the Rouergue menhir-statues.

In the sixth century BC, Celto-Iberian tribes occupied the camp at Ensérune. At the same time, the Greeks, having founded Phocaea (Marseille), settled in Agde, where their graceful bronzes bear witness to their prodigious talent as sculptors. Narbonne, the first town in Gaul to become Roman, prospered as the capital of Gallia Narbonensis at the crossroads of the Via Domitia and the Aquitaine Way. In the following centuries, successive invasions by Vandals, Visigoths, Saracens and the kings of Majorca were to leave their traces in local art and traditions.

Romanesque architecture flourished against the fine backdrop of the *garrigue* and the rugged mountains in the Pyrenees. In the tenth century the Roussillon acted as a cultural melting-pot, with influences converging from the east and the south. A primitive type of art emerged, fine examples of which can be seen in the lintels of the churches

at St-Génis-des-Fontaines and St-André-de-Sorrède and in the capitals of the cloisters at Elne. The tribune in the austere priory at Serrabone in the *garrigue* comes as a great surprise. This gem of finely chiselled – rather than carved – pink Roussillon marble, illustrating St John's Apocalypse, has wonderful stylized eagles, griffins and Oriental lions.

Not far away, in the monastery of St-Michel-de-Cuxa, Visigothic influences may be seen in the horseshoe-shaped arches in the transept of the abbey church. The cloisters have been reconstituted, in spite of some of the capitals having been removed to The Cloisters Museum in New York – a fate shared by the abbey of St-Guilhem-le-Désert near Montpellier. The long uphill climb through chestnut trees is rewarded by the stunning sight of the abbey of St-Martin-de-Canigou. The buildings, which are perched on a rock above a 1,094-metre drop, were ingeniously constructed to follow the lie of the land. The square bell-tower, with its ornamental arcading and Lombard bands, is similar to that of St-Michel-de-Cuxa.

Cistercian architecture also has its famous monuments. Among them are the restored former Abbaye de Sylvanès, the large, pink stone Abbaye de Valmagne rising out of the Languedoc vineyards, and, most particularly, the Abbaye de Fontfroide nestling in the Corbières vineyards.

Both Conques and Moissac were used as stopovers by pilgrims on their way to Santiago de Compostela in Spain. The church of Ste-Foy in Conques, built in the late eleventh century, was modelled on its sister churches in the Auvergne, while the church of St-Pierre in Moissac, which dates from the same period, has an Aquitaine influence. The doorways of these two abbey churches are triumphs of Romanesque sculpture. The tympanum at Conques illustrates the Last Judgement, that at Moissac a vision of St John's Apocalypse – both themes relating to Christ's return at the end of the world. In Toulouse, the pilgrimage church of St-Sernin, the largest Romanesque basilica in the West, consists of a subtle mixture of brick and stone. Its octagonal bell-tower, with five levels of Romanesque arches which are mitre-shaped on the top two levels, became the model for many churches in the Tarn. Its cloisters unfortunately disappeared in the nineteenth century, but its admirable capitals have been preserved in the Musée des Augustins.

The Gothic style, which reached the Midi in the late thirteenth century, retained much of the Romanesque. The brick churches still had a single broad aisle, bordered by small side chapels, which gave enough space for the gathering of great crowds. This was an important factor in the religious fervour of the twelfth and thirteenth centuries

(*OPPOSITE*) *Tympanum of the Church of St-Pierre, Moissac. Christ in majesty is surrounded by symbols of the Evangelists and the twenty-four Elders of the Apocalypse.*

(*LEFT*) *Eleventh-century cloister of St-Pierre, Moissac.*

(*ABOVE*) *One of St-Pierre's cloister pillars, representing an angel.*

(TOP) *Pont Vieux on the river Tarn at Albi.*

(ABOVE) *Private houses overlooking the Garonne, Toulouse.*

(RIGHT) *View of the fifteenth-century painting of the Last Judgement, and the organ, in Ste-Cécile Cathedral, Albi. The vault was decorated with frescoes by artists from Bologna in Italian Renaissance style.*

(OPPOSITE) *'Palm-tree' vaulting in the church of Les Jacobins, Toulouse.*

Towns and painters

when sermons, delivered mainly by the Mendicant orders such as the Franciscans, Dominicans and Jacobins, were much in demand. The most outstanding of these churches is the Cathédrale Ste-Cécile in Albi, which was built as a fortress just after the annihilation of the Cathars – the sectarians challenging the established Catholic Church. The interior is surprisingly refined, with its beautiful vaults painted in the Italian style, and the magnificent fresco of the Last Judgement. In the church of Les Jacobins in Toulouse the nave is separated by seven columns, reaching up into 'palm-tree' vaulting of radiating arches of the chancel.

The frontier regions of Roussillon, Capcir and Cerdagne, which were very unstable until the signing of the Treaty of the Pyrenees between France and Spain in 1659, have some interesting examples of military architecture. Salses Fort, set in a hollow, is an attractive pink brick and sandstone building of harmonious design. The enormous fortress was built in 1497 for Ferdinand of Aragon, and remained in Spanish hands until the seventeenth century. The technical brilliance of its Spanish architect Ramírez was much admired by Vauban, who, two centuries later, built the austere fortified town of Mont-Louis to the south west.

THE towns of the Languedoc are built in the beautiful white limestone of the *causses*. The cosmopolitan charm of Montpellier, an important university town, lies in its seventeenth- and eighteenth-century townscape. Hidden behind the discreet façades of these private mansions are courtyards with theatrical staircases, balusters and loggias, also seen at Pézenas.

In the districts around the attractive towns of Albi, Montauban and Toulouse, the houses are pink. This is the result of the local brick, which is very different from that of northern France and is the distinguishing mark of Toulouse. Warm and gleaming in the Midi sun, it also stamps its mark on the noble exteriors of the great cathedrals of St-Sernin in Toulouse and Ste-Cécile in Albi.

Every town in the Midi has its native artist, sculptor or painter: Bazille in Montpellier, Rigaud in Narbonne, Maillol in Banyuls, Toulouse-Lautrec in Albi and Ingres in Montauban. Former bishops' palaces have been converted into museums to house their works. The Palais de la Berbie, in Albi, has a remarkable collection of Toulouse-Lautrec's low-life paintings; in Montauban, there are Ingres' superb fantasies; and in Castres, Goya's disturbing *Caprichos* etchings.

The Cathar heresy

THE hill-top Château de Peyrepertuse, a long stone construction looking like a boat that has run aground on a rocky ridge, faces the Château de Quéribus balanced on top of a rock. Between the two, in the Corbières hills, are the russet-coloured vineyards of Cucugnan, the village of Alphonse Daudet's celebrated priest. This fiercely beautiful landscape lies at the heart of Cathar territory. Other fortresses to the north and west, including Puivert, Puilaurens, Lastours and Montségur, stand proudly on rocky outcrops, recalling the epic events which ravaged the whole region for almost a century.

It all began in 1167, at the Council of St-Félix-Lauragais. Bishop Nicetas of Constantinople, inspired by the Bogol movement in Bulgaria, founded an alternative church that took its name from the Greek word *katharos*, meaning pure. The 'Cathar' doctrine was based on the principle of the total separation of good and evil, the belief that man should be freed from the material world governed by Satan, and his divine purity restored. The church, which was made up of adherents known as *perfecti,* as well as ordinary believers, took hold in the feudal states of Languedoc and Roussillon.

Fearing the spread of this religion, Pope Innocent III launched the Albigensian crusade in 1209 to stamp out the heresy. The Capetian monarchy quickly joined the Pope, believing the crusade could help annexe the feudal states of the south to the kingdom. Noblemen from the north of France were urged to take part, with promises that they would obtain the same indulgences as in a crusade to the Holy Land. Castles and towns in Cathar hands resisted at first, then fell one after the other. The troubles were marked throughout by tragic episodes including the sacking of Béziers, the fall of Carcassonne, the siege of Lavaur and finally, in 1244, the funeral pyre at Montségur in which four hundred Cathars chose to die rather than to retract their beliefs. What had begun as a war of religion ended as a political conquest that extended the royal kingdom.

Several centuries later, the struggle between Protestantism and Catholicism re-ignited after nearly a century of peaceful coexistence. In 1557, the Calvinists arrived in the south of France and settled in the Cévennes and around Montauban. In 1629, several years after the Edict of Nantes, the Edict of Grace was signed in Alès by Louis XII allowing the Protestants freedom to practise their religion. The reprieve was short-lived. In 1661, Louis XIV undertook a vigorous campaign against the reformed religion. All kinds of methods were used to obtain conversions, including the *dragonnade*, whereby troops quartered with Protestants could behave as though they were in conquered territory.

In 1685, the revocation of the Edict of Nantes was signed, and Protestants became outlawed. Churches were demolished and ministers forced to flee. Those who remained practised their creed in secret in the wild Cévennes countryside. As the harassment continued, the Abbot of Chayla, who had imprisoned several Protestants, was assassinated and the *camisards*, peasants who were familiar with the Cévennes, engaged in guerrilla warfare; it took more than 30,000 men to match 4,000 *camisards*. The Edict of Tolerance was finally signed by Louis XVI in 1787. Every year there is a large Protestant pilgrimage to Le Mas Soubeyran near Anduze in the Cévennes, which remains a strongly Protestant region.

(ABOVE) The keep of Arques in the Corbières hills.

(OPPOSITE, TOP) Château de Peyrepertuse.

(OPPOSITE, BOTTOM LEFT) An ironwork door.

(OPPOSITE, BOTTOM RIGHT) A chapel in Cerdagne.

(*ABOVE*) *In the* bastide *of St-Clar, the garlic capital of France, the bulbs are hung out to dry before being plaited together for the market.*

(*LEFT*) *In some villages you can still see yoked oxen.*

(*OPPOSITE*) *Hams drying in the open air on butchers' stalls take pride of place beside the* saucisse de Toulouse. *In the Languedoc, near Toulouse, cooked pork meats are used in the recipe for the famous* cassoulet de Castelnaudary.

Festivities and holidays

LOCAL festivals in Sète, Palavas and Agde are celebrated with happy and exciting water tournaments, in which teams try to unbalance their opponents by lunging at them with lances, as in medieval jousts. In the Roussillon, the Catalan dance, the *sardana,* forms a part of all ceremonies and is accompanied by trumpets, tambourines and double bass. On Sundays, the entire population is devoted to rugby, which might almost be described as the national sport if it had not come from the other side of the Channel. After the match the traditional celebration is a glass of Banyuls, followed by a *cassoulet,* particularly in Toulouse and Castelnaudary, or a *bouillinade,* a crayfish stew from the Catalan coast.

With its sun, love of festivals and wonderful countryside, this region is a particular favourite with holidaymakers. Here, a complete change of surroundings is guaranteed for anyone who chooses hiking, pony trekking or mountain-biking along the tracks which wind across the lonely stretches of the Aubrac, Mont Lozère or the *causses.* For those who like to be on the water, there are also house-boat holidays on the Canal du Midi, the remarkable technical achievement of Pierre-Paul Riquet completed in 1680.

Those in search of more strenuous activities can race through the Tarn gorges in canoes, climb down into caves and chasms with pot-holing equipment, or scale rock-faces to hurl themselves off parapets. Others may choose to lounge on long beaches of white sand. Local spas, such as Lamalou-les-Bains in the heart of the Caroux massif, Amélie-les-Bains, Molitg-les-Bains and Céret at the foot of the Pyrenees, and Balaruc on the coast, dispense the well-being of their curative waters in beautiful settings. Finally, in winter, cross-country skiers have a choice between the Aubrac and Mont Lozère, while downhill skiers can make for the slopes at Font-Romeu.

Provence,
Côte d'Azur,
Corsica

Generations of artists and crowds of holidaymakers
are attracted by the grandeur of nature and the
intense Mediterranean landscape.

As soon as the traveller from the north reaches the environs of Montélimar, he is struck by a sudden change of climate and scenery. For it is on this imagined line that Provence reveals the majestic and rebellious nature that marks it out from the rest of France.

Here the mistral, blowing from the north, breaks up the scudding clouds and the azure sky glows with light. Bare hills split into ravines and the lean, blood-red slopes of limestone ranges, like a gigantic skeleton, loom upward with imposing overhangs and jagged crests. Plants and trees bow their backs and hug the ground, defending themselves against rocks, drought and the arch enemy, fire. Pines disguised as parasols, trees with twisted trunks and waxy, atrophied foliage attest to the unrelenting ferocity of the fight – even tropical palms, aloes and agaves are forced to seek shelter. Undernourished and half-starved rivers confine themselves to backwaters and creeks; in just a matter of hours deluge-like rains produce torrents which carry banks of pebbles downstream and lay waste everything in their path.

The inhabitants of this region, conscious of the sheer power of the elements, have opted for compromise. Here you will find villages, clinging to acropolis-like summits, built to snatch the sun's warmth in winter and to protect against its heat in summer. Lower down, there are *oustau* or peasant farmhouses, hooded to the north, their doors and windows flung wide and their trellised vines facing the south. The people themselves speak a local dialect, which it is said 'you catch by being born around Marseille'; the stranger will pick up its resonant and heavily accented tones the very first time he sets foot on Provençal soil, near, say, Bollène or Pont-St-Esprit. It suggests a taste for the theatrical and a passion for extremes that are somehow matched by the surroundings.

In the Midi the visitor is struck by the immediate sense of having been transported somewhere totally different. The Mediterranean captivates the imagination. It heralds the Tropics and the southern seas; it conjures up the images of caravanserai and the aromas of spice; it feeds the maddest of projects. It is this sense of the exotic that makes its appeal to hordes of holidaymakers who head towards its summer resorts, and to thousands of others who come here in retirement to seek the dream of eternal rejuvenation.

(OPPOSITE, FROM TOP TO BOTTOM)
Dentelles de Montmirail; forest fire in the Lubéron; the perched village of Peillon.

(OPPOSITE) *Crimson-flanked hillsides, the ochres of Roussillon.*

A patchwork of landscapes

Pᴿᴼⱽᴱᴺᶜᴱ and the Riviera form the eastern prong of the warm 'crescent of light' that extends from the Basque country to the Ligurian riviera, cutting across southern France on its way. To the south is the Tyrrhenian sea and the Mediterranean; to the north, the Alps. This land is characterized by the criss-crossing of an infinite number of local *pays*, all with quite different faces and chequered histories, creating a jigsaw of small natural regions. Plains run into hills; low, hunched ranges are camouflaged beneath pine-woods set against soaring barriers of rock, such as Cézanne's favourite Montagne Ste-Victoire; lofty crystalline hill-tops jut out above bleak, flat limestone ranges; plunging gorges lead into broad valleys and tumbling waters into vast motionless lakes; lush green oases of crops contrast with waterless wildernesses and long beaches of fine sand with steep cliffs.

This mosaic continues into the detail of the rural landscape. Tilled farmland rubs shoulders, in true Mediterranean tradition, with scrub, mountain or forest pasture and woods. Lines of cypress hedges enclose the rich palette of colours that inspired Van Gogh and other painters: fields of wheat, melons, tomatoes, lettuces, strawberries, olive groves, vineyards and orchards of cherry, apricot and peach. Huge greenhouses full of carnations, gladioli and mimosas glint in the sun and in the hinterland the square plots of lavender provide a delicate touch of colour. You can still find, on the odd hill festooned with *restanques*, or terraces, traces of micro-associations of crops related to the *coltura promiscua* of Tuscany – the last pocket of resistance to the advances of modern farming. A journey across this sun-drenched province – for example, from Marseille to Carpentras, by way of Pertuis and Apt – would vividly illustrate these frequent and astounding changes of landscape.

A sumptuous palette of colour, heightened by the paintings of Cézanne, Van Gogh and other artists.

(ABOVE RIGHT) La Montagne Ste-Victoire, *by Cézanne.*

(OPPOSITE TOP) Abbaye de Sénanque, founded in 1148. The simplicity of the architecture lends itself to tranquillity and suits the abbey's secluded position.

The dawn of time

PROVENCE and the Riviera play host to a number of important landmarks in the prehistory of Western European civilization. In the Grotte du Vallonet (Roquebrune-Cap-Martin), the oldest certified cave-dwelling in Europe, knapped stone tools suggest that the earliest human presence dates back some 950,000 years. On the floor of the Grotte de l'Escale cave at St-Estève-Jeanson (Bouches-du-Rhône) there is evidence that Provençal man made use of fire at least 700,000 years ago.

A more recent, and startling, discovery was the carving and painting of animals by artists some 20,000 years ago in the Cosquer cave. This cathedral of prehistory today lies below sea-level at the foot of the Calanques massif. Ten or so millennia earlier, other people had covered these same walls with 'hand outlines', believed to be among the most ancient known wall decorations in the world.

The thousands of rock carvings hewn on *chiappes*, the slabs rubbed smooth by glacial erosion, in the Vallée des Merveilles in the Mercantour massif represent extraordinary messages to posterity. Most date to the Bronze Age and are thought to be a figurative or pictorial expression of ancient Ligurian cults. In the western reaches of Lower Provence, shortly before the Roman conquest, the Celto-Ligurians also developed their own original art, including the 'severed heads' in niches in the macabre portal of the Roquepertuse sanctuary.

Greek and Roman traditions

Provence and the Côte d'Azur both have an ancient urban tradition. Although the *castellaras* of the Ligurians and the Celtic *oppida* of Nages, St-Blaise and Entremont lent momentum to the establishment of a dense network of small towns (some walled, others not), it was the encroachment of the Greeks and, above all, the Romans that played the decisive role in the history of the region.

With Rome as a model, each town is endowed with prestigious public and private buildings.

Images of Roman Provence:

(FAR LEFT) Vaison.

(ABOVE) St-Rémy.

(LEFT) Arles.

(OPPOSITE) Pont du Gard.

The earliest permanent trading settlements on the Provençal coast were established by Greeks from Phocaea in Asia Minor. Once they had founded Massalia (Marseille) at the end of the seventh century BC, they set up a chain of trading-posts and depots all along the coast at Citharista (La Ciotat), Olbia (Hyères), Antipolis (Antibes), Nikê (Nice), and Monaco, although inland, at Glanum and Avignon for example, their colonial ventures were less ambitious. At Marseille, the Lacydon creek was fitted out as a harbour and the port quickly rose to become the trading hub of Western Europe. Making the most of its new sphere of influence, the indigenous people learned the techniques of viticulture and building, developed a trading economy based on the use of currency, and were introduced to the most sophisticated forms of art.

Whereas Greek culture had spread at a snail's pace, hampered by the hinterland, things moved rapidly under Roman influence – 'the legionary took over from the merchant'. The new guardians exercised a firm and systematic colonial will, as evidenced by the organization of southern Gaul into the Provincia Narbonensis, whence the name 'Provence'. The region soon became part and parcel of the Roman world, adopting its way of life and justifying Pliny's observation, 'not so much a Province as another Italy'. Roman Provence was overlaid with a dense and efficient network of thoroughfares, such as the Via Domitia, the Via Aurelia and the Via Agrippa. Today, many a national highway and departmental byway have made use of these routes.

The region underwent brisk urban development, with the establishment of the fortified camp of Aquae Sextiae (Aix-en-Provence), the settlement of veterans of the Second Legion in Orange, the Sixth Legion in Arles, and the Eighth in Fréjus, the construction of Colonia Julia Apta (Apt) and the development of the federate city of Vaison.

With Rome as the model, each town acquired prestigious public and private buildings. Some of them can still be seen in their monumental context, providing a solemn venue for numerous festivals held in them: theatres in Arles, Vaison and Orange, amphitheatres in Arles, Nîmes and Fréjus, municipal arches in Orange and Carpentras, the Maison Carrée in Nîmes – the best preserved of all Roman temples – and the Mausoleum of the Ancients in St Rémy. Aqueducts – both grandiose, like the Pont du Gard, and more modest – acted as vital water-bearers.

Some of the architecture, like the crypto-portico of Arles, the so-called 'Alpine Trophy' at La Turbie, and the industrial mill at Balbegal have no equivalent anywhere else in Gaul. Nîmes enjoyed the lavish generosity of the emperors Hadrian

and Antoninus Pius; Arles was a bustling port where the emperor frequently resided; and Aix was the splendid capital of eastern Narbonensis Secundus. All these towns reflected the imperial splendour.

The geography of holy places, the legal system and the Provençal language (a mixture of Latin and Celto-Ligurian, a form of which is still used in conversation today) are all greatly indebted to the early Roman influence. This legacy, which survived the subsequent invasions relatively unscathed, was to last for several centuries after the fall of the Roman Empire.

The Camargue

*The white horses of the Camargue;
marshlands; pink flamingos; the traditional
house of a* gardian.

THE flat land of the Camargue resembles an unfinished
world with no strict boundaries between water and land,
like an area on the brink of creation. This huge deltaic plain is
produced by the combined efforts of the river Rhône, the
Mediterranean and sundry winds.

Folds of silt, and offshore bars formed over thousands of
years as the result of epic water battles, have imprisoned
marshlands, ponds and lagoons that are now home to herons,
egrets and flamingos as well as many other forms of wildlife.
Everything is in a state of flux: as random storms whip up the
sea and rivers swell in a trice, landscapes become
metamorphosed. The Rhône has only been flowing down its
present course since the fifteenth century, and the coast is prey
to non-stop shifts responsible for the silting-up of Aigues-
Mortes, where the statue of St Louis IX reminds us that the
monarch set sail from here for the Crusades, and for the sea
now lapping at the feet of Saintes-Maries, banished in the
Middle Ages several miles from the shore.

Modern drainage operations may have helped the
cultivation of the land, but the Camargue's *terra firma* remains
largely a barren expanse of grasslands, its sea-grass and sea-
lavender punctuated by tamarisk thickets, on which the white
Camargue horses and the black bulls with lyre-shaped horns
form a strange chequerboard pattern. The *gardian*, Old
Europe's version of the cowboy, no longer appears in his
traditional attire, except at a livestock event such as the springtime *ferrade* when young bulls are branded. The *gardian's* typical
Camargue thatched and whitewashed dwellings are gradually
being turned into holiday homes.

Water, air and fire

THE inscription '*Eici l'aigo es d'or*' (here water is gold), carved on a monument to the river Durance, expresses the paramount importance of husbanding water in a region of, depending on the season, searing heat-waves, drought and torrential downpours. Water is the nourisher, the dowser of fire, but here it is a rare commodity, not least because the colander-like limestone plateaux soak it up. So, water commands a respect verging on devotion, especially when it re-emerges into the light of day after a mysterious subterranean absence in the form of a resurgent spring, as at Fontaine-de-Vaucluse, or as just an ordinary source. Legend brims with miraculous outpourings. At Cotignac (Var), for example, St Joseph is said to have saved a labourer prostrate with thirst by showing him how to make water spout from the ground. Even today, local spring water is usually reckoned to be better than tap water, and will certainly be served when neighbours share a *pastis*. Modern water systems now solve most critical shortages, but signs of the preoccupation with water are everywhere: in endless ramifications of irrigation channels, in tanks and pools and in the town and village fountains that are the pride and hub of southern life.

On a day when the mistral is blowing, dust swirls, eyes water, hair is dishevelled, clothes flap, doors and shutters bang, and chairs and tables are tossed head-over-heels; its squalls leave you breathless and its piercing cold chills you to the bone. Taking its name from *magistrau*, the Provençal word for master, the mistral is one of the three traditional banes of Provence, along with the *Parlement* and the river Durance. Whereas the *Parlement* came to an end with the Ancien Régime, and the river has been harnessed, the wind still whips through the Donzère gorge to sweep away everything else in its path. One might forgive the mistral its ferocity since it leaves the sky more luminous and the colours more iridescent but, in these drought-ridden parts, it has one unacceptable vice: it fans fire.

The indescribably terrible fires, which periodically lay waste the limestone forests of Lower Provence, Les Maures and l'Estérel, are nothing short of calamities.

(OPPOSITE) Fountains, the pride of local townspeople and the Midi's favourite meeting places.

(TOP RIGHT) Waterfall in the Verdon gorges.

(RIGHT) Fire, the traditional enemy of the Mediterranean forest.

Images of popular devotion

THE popular legend of the 'saints of Provence' claims that the south of France was evangelized by Christ's own disciples. According to this version, the three Marys, Lazarus and Martha, who with others had been driven out of Palestine after the Passion, miraculously drifted in a boat to the shores of the Camargue.

History, while recording the earliest groups of Christians being in Arles and Marseille in the second century AD, agrees that Christianity reached these parts early. This was undoubtedly the source of the keen attachment to the earliest days of religion, and the mythological depiction of this simple faith professed ever since by the ordinary people of Provence. The various places visited by the passing evangelists have become sacred. In Saintes-Maries-de-la-Mer, where the miraculous vessel is alleged to have run aground, effigies of these early saints are proudly borne along in the two great annual processions. The pilgrimage to the grotto of Ste-Baume, where Mary Magdalene did penance, is renowned throughout the Midi; and in Tarascon the victory of her sister, Martha, over the monstrous beast, the Tarasque, is commemorated in splendour.

Christmas is the major event in Provence's festive calendar. The family ritual is the *gros souper,* a feast rounded off by the famous thirteen desserts, and their promise of indigestion. Between the various dishes and courses, everyone inspects the Christmas crib and its cluster of houses, lovingly arranged by the *papé,* the head of the family, on a corner of the sideboard. Each year brings yet more colourful crib figures (the Provençal *santons* or little saints) devotedly bringing their offerings to the child-God. Few, however, could claim to follow the chronology of the scene, when real-life Caspars, Melchiors and Balthazars, all mysteriously arrived a few days ahead of time, are welcomed by the village mayor and priest – if they are not invited to a game of *pétanque.*

Upholders of tradition will still go to midnight mass to see the birth of Jesus re-enacted with feeling in villages along the old transhumance routes: in Les Baux-de-Provence a little cart, decorated with greenery and carrying a new-born lamb, is drawn into church by a ram and accompanied by shepherds. The *pastorales,* a dramatic form of the living crib inspired by Provençal Christmas carols that overlay the theme of the Nativity with puns and irreverent asides, are currently enjoying a popular theatrical revival.

Provence has some of the most outstanding examples of *ex-voto* devotional images in France. From the seventeenth century, these poignant tokens of thanksgiving were frequently fixed to the walls of sanctuaries like Notre-Dame-des Lumières at Goult, Notre-Dame-de-la-Garde in Marseille and the chapel of St Anne in St-Tropez.

Romanesque, Gothic and Baroque

The twelfth century saw a stunning architectural renaissance in Provence. In Languedoc, Lombardy and the Auvergne, churches sprang up everywhere. Remarkable for their stone-work, they combined the varied influences of Roman antiquity, from which they inherited the basilical plan and the sober interior decoration. The finest examples are St-Trophime in Arles, St-Gilles-du-Gard, St-Gabriel in Tarascon, the cathedral of Notre-Dame-des-Doms in Avignon, and the church at Thor. Of all the cloisters housing the finest sculptural works, those at St-Trophime, with its splendid corner pillars decorated with statues of saints, are the most outstanding. A Benedictine abbey was founded at Montmajour, and Cistercian ones at Sénanque, Silvacane and Le Thoronet, the three 'sister abbeys' hallmarked by the austerity and asceticism required by the rule drawn up by St Bernard of Clairvaux.

(OPPOSITE) The village of Les Baux-de-Provence, guardian of tradition.

(LEFT) Religious zeal and folklore at an annual procession at Saintes-Maries-de-la-Mer.

(ABOVE) The gardians, *cowboys of Old Europe.*

(ABOVE) Avignon's splendour, symbolized by the Palais des Papes, the ramparts and the Pont Bénézet.

(LEFT AND FAR LEFT) The rich architectural heritage of Fréjus and St-Rémy-de-Provence.

(OPPOSITE) Lively cafés on the Cours Mirabeau, doyen of France's 'urban promenades', Aix-en-Provence.

BAROQUE FANTASY IN
AIX-EN-PROVENCE.

The cathedral at Fréjus, together with its fine adjacent cloister, is an important example of early Gothic art in Provence. The city of Avignon came into its own when, in the early fourteenth century, it became the seat of the papal court, the splendours of which lasted for a hundred years. This 'second Rome' girded itself with walls, more decorative than practical, and filled up with monasteries, churches and chapels. Meanwhile, successive popes expanded the papal palace and embellished this Gothic building to rival any royal court in Christendom; it still contains the magnificent frescoes of Giovanetti. Another Gothic masterpiece is the great basilica in St-Maximin, a building suffused by light and influenced by Bourges.

Baroque art arrived early in Provence, with a hint of French classicism. In Aix, seat of the *Parlement* and the university, the ever-growing number of administrative offices swelled the ranks of a nobility by no means averse to a little finery. The city spread in the seventeenth century, with spacious *cours*: what is now the Cours Mirabeau was the first urban avenue in France. Elegant mansions, graceful squares and pretty fountains by architects and decorators such as Pavillon, the Pugets, Mignard, and Parrocel gave lustre to the city. On the Côte d'Azur, the Baroque is best represented in religious buildings, in Sospel, Menton, Monaco and Nice.

Picturesque hilltop villages

PROVENCE, and more particularly the *départements* of Alpes-Maritimes and the Var, have many outstanding examples of *villages perchés* or hilltop villages, including Le Castellet, Bonnieux, Gourdon, Les Baux-de-Provence, Gordes, Ramatuelle, Saorge, Èze, Peillon, Roquebrune and Gorbio. Perched on a pyramid-like crag or scaling a hillside, these old Provençal villages express an architecture dictated by the physical limitations of the terrain.

Much of their aesthetic charm derives from the winding maze-like alleyways, steep lanes punctuated by steps and stairways, meandering beneath a warren of vaulted passages and archways, lined with tall, narrow façades. The warm colour of the stone, the red, orange, and yellow plasterwork, the misty-grey, almond and lilac shutters and the crimson, pink and apricot roof tiles, all conjure up the palette of Matisse.

The central square, shaded by plane trees, is the meeting-place for the local population, where tongues are wagged and opinions voiced on the state of the village or the politics of the nation, either on the café terrace or during a leisurely game of *pétanque*.

The markets of Provence

THE bustling and colourful markets of Provence take place in cities large and small and are remarkable for the quality and variety of the produce on offer. You can always locate a market in full swing by the hubbub of conversation and the swelling of the crowd. Turning into some narrow lane, you will be met by a jumble of multicoloured awnings and stalls brimming with produce.

At the fishmonger's stall, sharp-eyed gilthead bream and sea bass, perfect for grilling, can be found beside scorpion-fish, pandora and tub gurnard, essential for a stunning *bouillabaisse,* the most famous of Provençal dishes. The grocer's stall gives off a whole range of pungent aromas: there are all kinds of olives from the green *picholines* and *belgentiéroises* to the black *tanches* from Nyons and Carpentras; the classic 'herbs of Provence' – savory, thyme, basil, the crucial ingredient of *pistou* soup, sage for *aigo boulido,* rosemary, fennel for fish dishes, marjoram, star of any game stew or *civet*; vats brimming with anchovies; and the dried fruits called *mendicants* (after the four Mendicant orders), as well as many other delicacies.

The confectioner's trestles groan beneath the weight of the treats on sale there: marzipan *calissons* sweets from Aix, hard mint *berlingots* from Carpentras, candied fruit from Apt, nougat from Montélimar, quince pastries and jams made of watermelon and fig.

A step farther, decorated with braids of garlic, the market-gardener's stand is a must for *ratatouille* connoisseurs with its onions, courgettes, aubergines, peppers and red tomatoes (the less ripe are used for *salade niçoise*). As for fruit, there is the difficult choice between

ripe, wrinkled melons and juicy vineyard peaches.

Beyond the flower-stalls' eye-catching carnations and gladioli, freshly brought in from Ollioules and Carqueiranne, is the display of local goods and handicrafts: household soap scented with olive oil from Marseille, aromatic essences from Grasse, capital of the perfume industry, red, indigo and saffron-yellow Provençal fabrics printed in Arles, Avignon and Tarascon, varnished earthenware jars made by the potters of Aubagne, Vallauris, Biot and Salernes, cork trays from Les Maures, mortars for pounding garlic, the essential ingredient of *aioli* and olive-wood salad bowls.

Making your way out from this unforgettable experience, you still have the chance to stop at the Provençal wine stand and admire the mouthwatering vintages from Cassis, Bandol, Tavel and Châteauneuf-du-Pape .

(OPPOSITE, ABOVE) Game of pétanque *in the central square.*

(OPPOSITE, BELOW) Sigale, a hilltop village, Alpes-Maritimes.

(ABOVE AND RIGHT) Endless temptation in the Provençal markets.

Grasse, the world-famous capital of the scent industry: petals of roses, jasmine, lilac, orange blossom and other fragrant flowers are the prime ingredients of precious essences and perfumes.

Marseille and its creeks

SELLING FISH ON THE QUAYSIDE,
MARSEILLE.

PROVENCE is a coastal land – not a maritime, sea-faring one – and its inhabitants are 'stubborn landlubbers'. The exception is Marseille, doyen of the French cities founded by sailors, which is barricaded behind an amphitheatre of bare stripped hills.

For centuries Marseille was the traditional port of the Orient and, more particularly, the most important berth in the Mediterranean. The city owes everything to the sea. It has always depended on international trade and its colourful population includes sailors, dockers and immigrants of all nationalities. To this day, it has kept a strong personality and its own distinct cultural identity, where the creative flow of avant-garde music, drama, and dance interact with tall stories and the cries of fishwives. The splendid anchorage of the old port is an essential port of call for tourists, who will certainly seek out the Bar de la Marine before taking a short trip on the ferry-boat, then strolling up La Canebière, emblem of the pulsating city, which, as everyone knows, 'stops at the end of the world'.

To the east of Marseille, the blinding white limestone coast is hewn by deep and narrow indentations or *calanques* – sheer creeks forming majestic mergers of sky, sea and rock. Enjoying an amazingly sheltered and mild climate, and as if engraved on a mineral backdrop, they offer small havens to fishing vessels. They have also long been a favourite place for the people of Marseille to set up small seaside homes, called *cabanons*, the size of pocket-handkerchiefs, often making use of the old fisherman's huts or *oustalets*.

(*OPPOSITE*) *La Canebière, meeting place for seafarers from all corners of the globe.*

(*ABOVE*) *The* calanques, *a majestic union of sea, sky and rock.*

(*RIGHT*) *The corniche des Maures at Le Lavandou.*

The Riviera

THE ALLURE OF LUXURY.

'Leave Paris, plant your cane in my garden and the next day, when you wake, you will see roses growing from it." (Alphonse Karr in St-Raphaël, end of the nineteenth century.

From Bandol to Menton, the deep blue sea laps against more than 300 kilometres of shoreline of unmatched beauty. Dark, crystalline capes and headlands combine with long, golden coves and a necklace of bewitching small islands, set against a backdrop of rugged Alpine folds plunging sheer towards the Riviera.

The Côte d'Azur does not, of course, officially begin until St-Raphaël, but the effects of the mild climate – it is virtually free of mistral and frost – the tyranny of the sun and the year-round holiday atmosphere can all be sensed along the shores of the Massif des Maures and even as far west as Cap Sicié, beyond Toulon.

English and Russian aristocrats and gentry – those winter 'swallows' for whom the most luxurious of palaces and the most eccentric of villas were built along these shores – formed the tourist avant-garde. After 1918, the fashion for summer tourism caught on, following the lead of the rich and titled who were so fond of taking the air in health resorts. It then soon spread west towards Juan-les-Pins, St-Tropez and other spots, bringing an energetic and exuberant night-crowd. More recently, the tourist revolution, combined with the vogue for sea-bathing and suntans, has unleashed swarms of summer visitors from all over Europe who rush south, invading towns and villages that have become transformed into throbbing holiday resorts, each outdoing the next in high-class amenities and elegance.

Nice, capital of the Côte d'Azur, and much sought after since the eighteenth century, stands in a position of great beauty. Its attractions are underlined by the sweep of the Baie des Anges, the grandeur of its famous Promenade des Anglais, the colourful charm of its old town, as well as its flower processions and famous carnival. Cannes, the old city of the abbots of Lérins where the aristocrats traditionally spent their winters, is one of the most highly rated tourist cities of Europe; for the annual international film festival it joins the film capitals of the world. Wedged into an amphitheatre of hills, Monaco has sprouted daring skyscrapers around Le Rocher, the rock on which the prince's palace is perched; it still has its famous casino in Monte-Carlo. Villefranche-sur-Mer and its beautiful fishing port, Roquebrune guarded by an amazing tenth-century fortress, Menton surrounded by orange and lemon trees and Hyères, host to Queen Victoria, are some of the Côte d'Azur's other wonderful resorts.

(OPPOSITE, ABOVE) Villa Île-de-France, St-Jean-Cap-Ferrat; a splendid eccentricity of the Belle Époque.

(OPPOSITE, BOTTOM LEFT) Terrace of the Hôtel Martinez, Cannes; a famous rendezvous during the international film festival.

(OPPOSITE, BOTTOM RIGHT) Coastline of the Esterel massif.

(RIGHT) Promenade des Anglais, Nice.

Corsica

PROCESSION AT CALVI.

MAGNIFICENT and rugged, Corsica – its name means rock – has forged its character in isolation. First Pisan, then Genoese before becoming French, this large Mediterranean island has managed to retain its own proud identity. The environment certainly has played its part. Even the relentlessly colonizing Romans were rebuffed by the maze of crests and ridges, the fantastic escarpments and the crazy ravines that characterize the landscape: the needles of Bavella and Cinto, the chaotic forms of La Castagniccia, the Dante-esque relief of the Piana inlet and the bottomless gorge of La Spelunca. Bridle-paths straddled by impossible humpback bridges were for long the island's only means of communication, for mules and photographers alike; today's paved roads, still narrow and winding, are their direct heirs. But those who take the time to explore will be rewarded. For as well as being the stereotyped island of the Emperor Napoleon and a few famous bandits, Corsica has an authentic civilization. This is underpinned by a rich and zestful language still used by the majority of Corsicans, and by religious and secular traditions that are still very much alive, such as the Good Friday procession keenly followed by women wearing the *mezzaro* (a kerchief knotted beneath the chin) or the performance of the *paghjella*, a poignant polyphonic chant.

Corsica is more mountain than island. For a long time turning inward rather than towards the sea, it boasts splendid shores, most of which remain untouched by unfortunate

development. A succession of beautiful beaches are lapped by clear Mediterranean waters, jagged headlands are still guarded by the towers of the Office of St George, and, within deep, rocky inlets, tiny sleepy harbours bask in the heat of the sun. One or two coastal towns are lively and commercial: the standard-bearer of Napoleonic fortunes, Ajaccio-la-Blanche, with its outstandingly mild climate; the citadel town of Calvi, where the Balagne hills descend to the sea; Bastia, the 'city of the Levant', whose old centre and picturesque port have managed to retain a typically Mediterranean feel; and Bonifacio, the impregnable Genoese fortress city, perched between sea and *garrigue* scrubland.

The interior, where the scenery is even more rugged, is full of surprises: stelae, still half-shrouded in mystery; small chapels with multi-coloured masonry-work rising out of the scrub; forests of beech and Corsican pine at Aïtone and Vizzavona; the Castagniccia chestnut woods miraculously unscathed by innumerable fires; the chain of lakes on Mont Rotondo; and the shady crag-top villages in the Nebbio and Balagne hills. Ancient walled cities are the very soul of Corsica. Corte, still redolent of its steely heroes Sampiero Corso, Gaffori and Pascal Paoli, is one example; another is Sartène, perhaps the most Corsican of all Corsican towns.

(ABOVE) Piana inlet.

(LEFT) Bonifacio's proud citadel.

(OPPOSITE) A succession of superb beaches and jagged promontories in the Gulf of Porto.

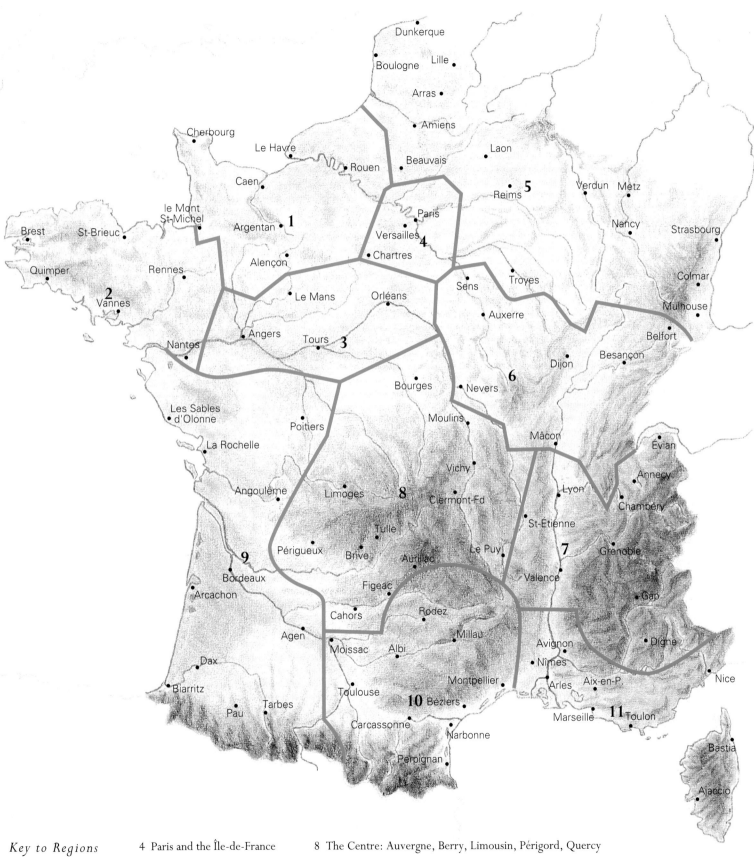

Dunkerque
Boulogne • Lille
Arras
• Amiens
Cherbourg
Le Havre • Laon
Caen Rouen Beauvais 5 Verdun Metz
le Mont Paris Nancy Strasbourg
St-Michel Argentan 1 Versailles 4
Alençon Chartres Colmar
Brest St-Brieuc Troyes Mulhouse
Rennes Le Mans Orléans Sens
Quimper Auxerre Belfort
2 Vannes Angers Tours 3
Nantes Bourges Nevers 6 Dijon Besançon
Les Sables Moulins
• d'Olonne Poitiers Mâcon
La Rochelle Évian
Vichy Lyon Annecy
Angoulême Limoges 8 Clermont-Fd Chambéry
Tulle St-Étienne 7 Grenoble
9 Périgueux Brive Le Puy
Bordeaux Aurillac Valence Gap
Arcachon Figeac
Cahors Rodez Digne
Agen Millau Avignon
Dax Moissac Albi Nîmes Aix-en-P. Nice
Biarritz Toulouse 10 Béziers Arles 11 Toulon
Pau Tarbes Marseille
Carcassonne Narbonne
Perpignan
Bastia

Ajaccio

Key to Regions | 4 Paris and the Île-de-France | 8 The Centre: Auvergne, Berry, Limousin, Périgord, Quercy
1 Normandy | 5 The North and East | 9 The Atlantic Coast
2 Brittany | 6 Burgundy and Franche-Comté | 10 Languedoc and Midi-Pyrenees
3 The Loire Valley | 7 Rhône-Alps | 11 Provence, Côte d'Azur, Corsica

Acknowledgements

The publisher thanks the photographers and organizations for their kind permission to reproduce the following photographs in this book:

1 Agence Top/Marie-José Jarry/Jean-François Tripelon; 2-3 Serge Chirol; 6-7 Gilles Rigoulet; 8-9 Agence Top/Rosine Mazin; 10 left Christian Sarramon; 10 centre Agence Top/Rosine Mazin; 10 right Guy Bouchet; 10-11 Cyril le Tourneur-d'Ison; 12 above left Agence Top/Daniel CZAP; 12 above right Agence Top/Pierre Hussenot; 12 below Agence Top/Rosine Mazin; 13 Robert Harding Picture Library/L Bond; 14 Michael Holford; 14-15 Gilles Rigoulet; 16 VISA/A Venturi; 17 above John Sims; 17 centre Cyril le Tourneur-d'Ison; 17 below Christian Sarramon; 18 above left Agence Top/Guy Bouchet; 18 above right Gilles Rigoulet; 18 centre Guy Bouchet; 18 below Magnum/Dennis Stock; 18-19 Laurence Delderfield; 20-21 Gilles Rigoulet; 21 above Serge Chirol; 21 below Serge Chirol; 22 above Christian Sarramon; 22 below left Scope/Jacques Guillard; 22 below right Explorer/Luc Girard; 23 above Jean-Loup Charmet; 23 below left Agence Top/Guy Bouchet; 23 below right Agence Top/Rosine Mazin; 24 above Robert Harding Picture Library/Ken Gillham; 24 below Explorer/P Roy; 25 Explorer/Antonio Autenzio; 26 Bridgeman Art Library/Lauros-Giraudon/Musée d'Orsay; 26-27 Serge Chirol; 28 left Serge Chirol; 28 centre Joe Cornish; 28 right Agence Top/Pierre Hussenot; 28-29 Laurence Delderfield; 30 Guy Bouchet; 31 above Agence Top/H A Segalen; 31 below left John Sims; 31 below right Explorer/J Dupont; 32 above Agence Top/Guy Bouchet; 32 below Serge Chirol; 33 above left Explorer/N Thibaut; 33 below left Explorer/Jean Desmarteau; 33 right Gilles Rigoulet; 34 above Bernard Bardinet; 34 below Gilles Rigoulet; 34-35 Gilles Rigoulet; 36-37 Guy Bouchet; 37 Explorer/Guy Thouvenin; 38 left Magnum/Bruno Barbey; 38 right John Sims; 38-39 Magnum/Bruno Barbey; 39 Serge Chirol; 40 above Robert Harding Picture Library/Adam Woolfitt; 40 below Cyril le Tourneur-d'Ison; 41 left Agence Top/Hervé Champollion; 41 above right DIAF/D Somelet; 41 below right Serge Chirol; 42-45 Joe Cornish; 46 Bridgeman Art Library/Giraudon/Musée d'Orsay (Yellow Haystacks by Paul Gauguin); 47 above Bridgeman Art Library/Worthing Museum and Art Gallery (The Laundry at St Nicolas du Pelem, Brititany by Stanislawa de Karlowska); 47 below ET Archive (Breton Women with Umbrellas, Emile Bernard, © DACS 1995); 48-49 Images/Granville Harris; 49 left Serge Chirol; 49 right Michael Busselle; 50 above Michael Busselle; 50 below Explorer/B Rebouleau; 51 Robert Harding Picture Library/Adam Woolfitt; 52 above left Explorer/H Veiller; 52 above right Explorer/N Thibaut; 52 below Serge Chirol; 52-53 Michael Busselle; 54 Scope/Jean-Daniel Sudres; 54-55 Scope/Michel Guillard; 56 above Serge Chirol; 56 below left Explorer/J P Champroux; 56 below right Agence Top/Rosine Mazin; 57 Gilles Rigoulet; 58 Agence Top/Rosine Mazin; 59 left Explorer/F Jalain; 59 right Agence Top/Catherine Bibollet; 60 above Daniel & Emmanuelle Minassian; 60 below Laurence Delderfield; 60-61 Joe Cornish; 61 above VISA/A Zezmer; 61 below Joe Cornish; 62 above Explorer/J-L de Laguarigue; 62 below VISA/C Sappa; 62-63 VISA/C Sappa; 64-65 Serge Chirol; 65 Joe Cornish; 66 above left Michelle Garrett; 66 above right Anne Gaël; 66 below VISA/C Rives; 66-67 André Martin; 67 Explorer/A E Guillou; 68 above Patrick Eagar; 68 below Agence Top/J Ducange; 69 Michael Busselle; 70 left Matthew Weinreb; 70 centre Christian Sarramon; 70 right Matthew Weinreb; 70-71 Robert Harding Picture Library/Explorer; 72 above Matthew Weinreb; 72 below left DIAF/Moirenc; 72 below right Guy Bouchet; 73 Frank Spooner Pictures/Gamma/Eric Sander; 74 above Hutchison Library/Bernard Régent; 74 below Joe Cornish; 75 above Matthew Weinreb; 75 below Explorer/A Autenzio/E.P.G.L. Architect I M Pei; 76 left Serge Chirol; 76 right Explorer/Henri Veiller; 76-77 Serge Chirol; 77 Robert Harding Picture Library/Explorer; 78 Explorer/Pierre Tetrel; 78-79 DIAF/G Guittot; 80 Matthew Weinreb; 81 above Matthew Weinreb; 81 below Guy Bouchet; 82 above DIAF/Daniel Thierry; 82 centre Christian Sarramon; 82 below left Archipress/S Couturier; 82 below right Christian Sarramon; 82-83 Bridgeman Art Library /Private Collection (Paris Street Scene, Jean Beraud ©ADAGP, Paris & DACS, London 1995); 83 left Christian Sarramon; 83 below Magnum/ Steele Perkins; 84 Explorer/D Clement; 85 left Gilles Rigoulet; 85 above right Matthew Weinreb; 85 below right Christian Sarramon; 86 left Gilles Rigoulet; 86 right Joe Cornish; 86-87 Hutchison Library/Chris Johnson; 87 Guy Bouchet; 88 above left Matthew Weinreb; 88 above right Magnum/ Fred Mayer; 88 below left Rex Features/SIPA Press/E Malanca; 88 below right Frank Spooner Pictures/Paul Massey; 89 above left Christian Sarramon; 89 above right Agence Top/Marie-José Jarry/Jean-François Tripelon/ © Eclairage SNTE; 89 below left Matthew Weinreb; 89 below right Magnum/Fred Mayer; 90 above Guy Bouchet; 90 below left Robert O'Dea; 90 below right Serge Chirol; 91 Christian Sarramon; 92 above left Archipress/L Boegly; 92 above right Joe Cornish; 92 centre Christian Sarramon; 92 below Joe Cornish; 93 VISA/W Louvet; 94 Agence Top/Hervé Champollion; 95 above left Christian Sarramon; 91 above right Guy Bouchet; 95 below left Gilles Rigoulet; 95 below centre Frank Spooner Pictures/Gamma/Castro; 95 below right Guy Bouchet; 96-97 Gilles Rigoulet; 97 left Robert Harding Picture Library/Adam Woolfitt; 97 centre Robert Leslie; 97 right Robert Leslie; 98 Explorer/H Donnezan; 99 above David Hughes; 99 below Michael Busselle; 100-101 Michael Busselle; 101 above Gilles Rigoulet; 101 centre Explorer/J P Lescourret; 101 below Gilles Rigoulet; 102 DIAF/Thomas Jullien; 103 above Christophe Boisvieux; 103 below left Gilles Rigoulet; 103 below right Gilles Rigoulet; 104 above left Archipress/L Boegly; 104 above right Agence Top/Rosine Mazin; 104 below Explorer/René Mattes; 105 Archipress/Luc Boegly; 106-107 Gilles Rigoulet; 107 above Robert Harding Picture Library/Adam Woolfitt; 107 below Christian Sarramon; 108 left Serge Chirol; 108 right Laurence Delderfield; 109 Serge Chirol; 110 Archipress/Marc Loiseau; 111 above left Christian Sarramon; 111 above right Archipress/M Loiseau; 111 below Explorer/P Broquet; 112 above Explorer/Dominique Reperant; 112 below DIAF/Ouzounoff; 113 left Francesco Venturi/KEA; 113 right J-P Dumontier; 114 Michael Busselle; 115 above Michael Busselle; 115 below left Serge Chirol; 115 below right Serge Chirol; 116 left Explorer/M Cambazard; 116 right Explorer/P Thomas; 117 Gilles Rigoulet; 118 above André Martin; 118 below left Anthony Blake Picture Library; 118 below right DIAF/J P Langeland; 119 Robert Leslie; 120-121 Explorer/Erik Sampers; 121 left André Martin; 121 centre Christophe Boisvieux; 121 right Explorer/P Lorne; 122 above Bernard Bardinet; 122 below Guy Bouchet; 122-123 Christophe Boisvieux; 124 above Magnum/Eric Lessing; 124 below Serge Chirol; 125 Explorer/A Wolf; 126 Explorer/Paul Wysocki; 127 above Explorer/Francis Jalain; 127 below left Bridgeman Art Library/Musée Condé, Chantilly (September: the beating of walnuts and grape harvest Hours of the Duchess of Burgundy); 127 below right Serge Chirol; 128 left Serge Chirol; 128 right Agence Top/Alain Rivière-Lecoeur; 129 Christian Sarramon; 130 above Agence Top/Hervé Champollion; 130 below left Guy Bouchet; 130 below right Christophe Boisvieux; 131 above Serge Chirol; 131 below Serge Chirol; 132 Michael Busselle; 133 above André Martin; 133 below Explorer/Dominique Reperant; 134 above Explorer/E Sampers; 134 below Impact/John Sims; 134-135 Christophe Boisvieux; 135 Explorer/M Plassart; 136 above left Michael Busselle; 136 below left Laurence Delderfield; 136 above right Michael Busselle; 136 below right Laurence Delderfield; 137 Agence Top/Alain Rivière-Lecoeur; 138 above Serge Chirol; 138 below left Explorer/H Veiller; 138 below right Agence Top/Robert Tixador; 139 John Sims; 140 Anne Gaël; 141 above Explorer/F Jalain; 141 below Magnum/Richard Kalvar; 142-143 John Cleare Mountain Camera; 143 left Rex Features/SIPA Press/Jean Clottes; 143 centre VISA/F Vasseur; 143 right Gilles Rigoulet; 144 above left Michael Busselle; 144 above right André Martin; 144 centre Serge Chirol; 144 below David Ward; 145 David Ward; 146-147 Gilles Rigoulet; 147 left Gilles Rigoulet; 147 right Robert Harding Picture Library/Loraine Wilson; 148 above André Martin; 148 below Bernard Bardinet; 148-149 Michael Busselle; 149 above Gilles Rigoulet; 149 below left Robert Leslie; 149 below right Archipress/Alain Goustard/Architects Groupe 6; 150 Images/Joe Cornish; 151 above John Sims; 151 below left Agence Top/Daniel Gleitz; 151 below right Images Photothèque/Noval; 152-153 Jerrican/Transglobe/T Kruger; 154 VISA/Alfredo Venturi; 154-155 VISA/B Rajau; 155 above VISA/Afredo Venturi; 155 below Scope/Jacques Sierpinski; 156-157 Hutchison Library/Bernard Régent; 157 left Hutchison Library/Bernard Régent; 157 above right Hutchison Library/Bernard Régent; 157 centre right Archipress/Stephane Couturier; 157 below right Archipress/Stephane Couturier; 158 above Christian Sarramon; 158 below left Christian Sarramon/Architect Jean Nouvel; 158 below right Gilles Rigoulet/Architect Jean Nouvel; 159 above Christian Sarramon; 159 below Archipress/S Couturier; 160 Christian Sarramon; 161 above David Ward; 161 below Impact/Cedri/Liebaux; 162 above Serge Chirol; 162 below Scope/Michel Guillard; 163 Michael Busselle; 164-165 Cosmos/François Perri; 165 left Images Photothèque/Erskine; 165 right Cosmos/François Perri; 166 Impact/David Gallant; 166-167 Agence Top/Rosine Mazin; 167 above Explorer/J Damase; 167 below Michael Busselle; 168 above Explorer/Dominique Reperant; 168 below left Explorer/J B Lafitte; 168 below right Explorer/F Jalain; 169 above Images Photothèque/Le Naviose; 169 below Explorer/Dominique Reperant; 170 Serge Chirol; 170-171 Images Photothèque/Le Naviose; 171 left VISA/S Marmounier; 171 right Images Photothèque/Le Naviose; 172 Explorer/A Bordes; 173 above left Explorer/Joel Damase; 173 above right Scope/Jean-Daniel Sudres; 173 below Scope/Jean-Daniel Sudres; 174-175 Jerrican/Labat; 175 above Explorer/P Broquet; 175 centre Serge Chirol; 175 below Guy Bouchet; 176 above Explorer/D Reperant; 176 below left VISA/J Schurr; 176 below right Serge Chirol; 176-177 Explorer/J P Lescourret; 178 above Scope/Michel Guillard; 178 below Benard Bardinet; 179 above left Michael Busselle; 179 below left Images Photothèque/Pleuriot; 179 above right Bernard Bardinet; 179 below right Michael Busselle; 180 above James Davis Travel Photography; 180 below Christian Sarramon; 181 above Christian Sarramon; 181 below Agence Top/Marie-José Jarry/Jean-François Tripelon; 182 above Serge Chirol; 182 below Serge Chirol; 182-183 Michael Busselle; 184 left Images Photothèque/Carcanague-Obellianne; 184 right Explorer/Gary Sommer; 185 Explorer/S Grandadam; 186-187 Robert Harding Picture Library/Explorer; 187 left Guy Bouchet; 187 centre Jerrican/Ch Errath; 187 right Scope/Jean-Luc Borde; 188 above left Magnum/Bruno Barbey; 188 above right Jerrican/Ch Errath; 188 centre Michael Busselle; 188 below Christian Sarramon; 189 Explorer/Francis Jalain; 190 left Guy Bouchet; 190 above right Explorer/Jean-Franco Pernetto; 190 below right VISA/A Lorgnier; 191 Christian Sarramon; 192 left Christian Sarramon; 192 right Scope/Jean-Luc Bardre; 193 left Agence Top/Marie-José Jarry/Jean-François Tripelon; 193 above right Magnum/Guy le Querrec; 193 below right Images Photothèque/Carcanague; 194 above Agence Top/Marie-José Jarry/Jean-François Tripelon; 194 below left Agence Top/Rosine Mazin; 194 below centre Jerome Darblay; 194 below right Christian Sarramon; 195 above J-P Dumontier; 195 below Christian Sarramon; 196 above Serge Chirol; 196 below Images Photothèque/Teissedre; 196-197 Hutchison Library/Bernard Régent; 197 Serge Chirol; 198 Michael Busselle; 199 above Robert Harding Picture Library/Explorer; 199 below Michael Busselle; 200 above Images Photothèque/Laurence Delderfield; 200 below left Robert Harding Picture Library/Adam Woolfitt; 200 below right Images Photothèque/Delderfield; 200-201 Rex Features/Martin Richard; 201 Bernard Bardinet; 202-203 Christian Sarramon; 203 Christian Sarramon; 204-205 Images Photothèque/Carcangue; 205 above Explorer/F Jalain; 205 centre John Cleare Mountain Camera/Peter Smith; 205 below Scope/Jean-Daniel Sudres; 206 Jean-Pierre Godeaut; 207 above left Laurence Delderfield; 207 below left Jean-Pierre Godeaut; 207 right Cephas Picture Library/Mick Rock; 208-209 Cyril le Tourneur-D'Ison; 209 left Images Photothèque/ Cartier; 209 centre Images Photothèque/Nimetz; 209 right Images Photothèque/Dumas; 210 Serge Chirol; 211 left Anne Gaël; 211 above right Images Photothèque/Perrine; 211 below right Anne Gaël; 212 Robert Harding Picture Library/ Adam Woolfitt; 212 right Laurence Delderfield; 213 above Images Photothèque/Angers; 213 below left Cyril le Tourneur-d'Ison; 213 below right Serge Chirol; 214 above Bridgeman Art Library/Hermitage, St Petersburg (View of Collioure by Henri Matisse, © Succession H Matisse/DACS 1995); 214 below left DIAF/Jean Gabanou; 214 below right DIAF/D Leraul; 215 above Antoinè Rozes; 215 below Images Photothèque/Dumas; 216 Images Photothèque/ Carcanague ; 217 left Serge Chirol; 217 right Images Photothèque/Carcanague; 218 above left Explorer/ D Reperant; 218 below left Explorer/Guy Thouvenin; 218 right Christian Sarramon; 219 Images Photothèque/Novali; 220 Serge Chirol; 221 above Christophe Boisvieux; 221 below left Anne Gaël; 221 below right Cyril le Tourneur-d'Ison; 222 above Michael Busselle; 222 below Explorer/L Girard; 223 Explorer/F Jalain; 224-225 Michael Busselle; 225 left DIAF/Daniel Thierry (Statue, Jeune Fille S'Evadant by Joan Miro © ADAGP, Paris and DACS, London); 225 centre DIAF/J-Ch Gerard; 225 right Stephane Frances; 226 above Vincent Motte; 226 centre Michael Busselle; 226 below Explorer/D Reperant; 227 Vincent Motte; 228 above left Vincent Motte; 228 below left Vincent Motte; 228 below right Magnum/Dennis Stone; 228-229 Bridgeman Art Library/Hermitage, St Pétersburg (Mont St Victoire by Paul Cezanne); 229 top right Agence Top/Hervé Champollion; 229 above right Explorer/M Breton; 229 centre right Vincent Motte; 229 below left Scope/Daniel Faure; 229 below centre Images Photothèque/J Boyer; 229 below right Christian Sarramon; 230 left Anne Gaël; 230 above right DIAF/J Ch Gerard; 230 below right Explorer/A Roux; 231 DIAF/Gerard Gsell; 232 DIAF/Camille Moirenc; 232-233 Explorer/G Martin-Ragett; 233 above DIAF/J C Pratt/D Pries; 233 centre Explorer/G Martin-Ragett; 233 below Scope/Jean-Daniel Sudres; 234 above left Jerrican/Noodles; 234 below centre Jerrican/Roland; 234 below left DIAF/Moirenc; 234 above right DIAF/J-Ch Gerard; 234 centre right Michael Busselle; 234 below right Louisa Jones; 235 above Images Photothèque/Noval; 235 below Images Photothèque/Laporte; 236 above DIAF/J P Garcin; 236 below Explorer/Dominique Reperant; 237 above Explorer/Y Cavaille; 237 above DIAF/J-P Garcin; 238 above DIAF/J-P Garcin; 238 below left DIAF/Thierry Leconte; 238 below right Michael Busselle; 239 above Images Photothèque/ Delderfield; 239 below DIAF/Moirenc; 240 above Images Photothèque/Cercanague; 240 below H Wysocki; 241 above Agence Top/Marie-José Jarry/Jean-François Tripelon; 241 below Agence Top/Marie-José Jarry/Jean-François Tripelon; 242-243 André Martin; 243 above DIAF/J-C Gerard; 243 centre left André Martin; 243 centre right DIAF/J-Ch Gerard; 243 below Explorer/J P Nacivet; 244 above Magnum/Abbas; 244 below DIAF/J-P Garcin; 245 above Jerrican/Zintzmeyer; 245 below Stephane Frances; 246 above Stephane Frances; 246 below left Stephane Frances; 246 below right Michael Busselle; 247 above Stephane Frances; 247 below Agence Top/Marie-José Jarry/Jean-François Tripelon; 248 above left Christian Sarramon; 248 above right Christophe Boisvieux; 248 below VISA/A Lorgnier; 249 Serge Chirol; 250 Michael Busselle; 253 Archipress/S Courtier.

Index

Page numbers in *italic*
denote illustrations